Fouad ben Nasr Omri

Weighted Statistical Testing based on Active Learning and Formal Verification Techniques for Software Reliability Assessment

The Karlsruhe Series on Software Design and Quality
Volume 22

Chair Software Design and Quality
Faculty of Computer Science
Karlsruhe Institute of Technology

and

Software Engineering Division
Research Center for Information Technology (FZI), Karlsruhe

Editor: Prof. Dr. Ralf Reussner

Weighted Statistical Testing based on Active Learning and Formal Verification Techniques for Software Reliability Assessment

by

Fouad ben Nasr Omri

KIT Scientific Publishing

Dissertation, Karlsruher Institut für Technologie
KIT-Fakultät für Informatik

Tag der mündlichen Prüfung: 16. Juli 2015
Gutachter: Prof. Dr. Ralf Reussner, Prof. Dr. Bernhard Beckert

Impressum

KIT Scientific Publishing

Karlsruher Institut für Technologie (KIT)
KIT Scientific Publishing
Straße am Forum 2
D-76131 Karlsruhe

KIT Scientific Publishing is a registered trademark
of Karlsruhe Institute of Technology.
Reprint using the book cover is not allowed.

www.ksp.kit.edu

Print on Demand 2018 – Gedruckt auf FSC-zertifiziertem Papier

ISSN 1867-0067
ISBN 978-3-7315-0472-6
DOI: 10.5445/KSP/1000051517

Abstract

Our society relies on the correct functioning of software systems and their failures can result in humanitarian and financial damages. Hence, a high confidence of the reliability of software systems is usually required. Existing software reliability assessment approaches are either theoretical sound but time-consuming and labor-intensive (huge number of test cases, proof conduction, etc.), or practical but based on unrealistic assumptions and usually deliver overestimation of the reliability. For ultra-high reliable software systems, like for example flight control systems, a failure rate of 10^{-9} with a confidence of at least 99.99% is usually required. This means that at least $9,210,340,628$ failure-free test cases should be executed to assess such a reliability requirement. If we assume that we can execute 10 test cases per second, this would mean that a total of $10,660$ days of testing are required. This obviously prohibitively impractical and impossible. We think that our approach is the right direction to make the assessment of ultra-high reliable software possible.

This thesis developed an automatic approach for the assessment of software reliability which is both theoretical sound and practical. The developed approach extends and combines theoretical sound approaches in a novel manner to systematically reduce the overhead of reliability assessment.

More precisely, the developed approach formulates software reliability assessment as an uncertainty reduction approach about the unknown reliability of the software. Existing approaches are assessing the software reliability without making use of the information available from previous test executions, the software source code or previous proof of correctness attempts. The presented approach, however, formulates such available information as prior knowledge and uses such knowledge to systematically reduce the overhead of software reliability assessment by reducing the required number of test cases executions to reach a target confidence on the reliability estimate.

This thesis makes the following statements: available knowledge about the failure rate of the software should reduce uncertainty about its future reliability and hence reduce the required overhead to assess it.

The approach makes use of previous black-box test cases executions to optimally select the future test cases to execute in order to reach a target confidence on the reliability estimate with less test cases than state-of-art approaches. If the source code of the software under study is available, the approach uses the information provided by the source code to further reduce the required number of test cases. If a proof of correctness of the source code or parts of it has been conducted, the approach make use of the confidence gained by the proof to further reduce the required testing overhead.

Software reliability assessment based on testing executes test cases with respect to an operational profile, which is a quantitative approximation of the software's operational use. The reliability estimation is usually sensitive to variations of the operational profile. We show how our approach can reduce such sensitivity based on variance reduction and systematic software input domain pruning.

The approach has been validated on several case studies. The validation shows the efficiency of the approach compared to state-of-the-art techniques to reduce the overhead required for software reliability assessment.

Kurzfassung

Heutzutage ist unsere Gesellschaft sehr abhängig von der korrekten Funktion von Softwaresystemen. Ein Software-Ausfall könnte zu humanitären und finanziellen Schäden führen. Daher ist in der Regel ein hohes Maß an Konfidenz der Zuverlässigkeit von Softwaresystemen erforderlich. Die bestehenden Bewertungsansätze der Software-Zuverlässigkeit sind entweder theoretisch fundiert aber sehr aufwendig oder praxisnah aber basierend auf unrealistische Annahmen.

Diese Doktorarbeit entwickelt einen automatischen Ansatz für die theoretisch fundierte und gleichzeitig praxisnahe Bewertung der Software-Zuverlässigkeit. Der entwickelte Ansatz erweitert und verbindet solide theoretische Ansätze in einer Art und Weise, um den Aufwand der Zuverlässigkeitsbewertung systematisch und sukzessive zu reduzieren.

Diese Dissertation macht die folgende Aussage: jedes Wissen über die Ausfallrate der Software soll die Unsicherheit bez. der Zuverlässigkeit reduzieren, und damit minimiert es den Aufwand sie zu bewerten. Der Ansatz nutzt frühere Ausfürungen von Black-Box-Testfällen, um die zukünftigen Testfälle optimal zu wählen. Ziel ist es, die Zuverlässigkeit mit weniger Testfällen als Stand-der-Technik-Verfahren zu erreichen. Ist der Quellcode der Software vorhanden, dann nutzt der Ansatz die Informationen aus dem Quellcode aus, um die erforderliche Anzahl von Testfällen weiter zu reduzieren. Falls der Quellcodes oder Teile davon formal verifiziert wurden, nutzt der Ansatz die aus dem Beweis erlangte Konfidenz zur weiteren Reduzierung des erforderlichen Testaufwands.

In der Regel reagiert die Zuverlässigkeitsschätzung empfindlich auf Schwankungen des Benutzungsprofils. Wir zeigen, dass unser Ansatz solch eine Empfindlichkeit basierend auf Varianzreduktion und systematischer Reduzierung des Eingaberaum reduzieren kann.

Wir haben unseren Ansatz anhand mehrerer Fallstudien validiert.

Acknowledgements

First, I wish to thank my advisor Prof. Dr. Ralf Reussner for his support, understanding and encouragement during my Ph.D. Prof. Dr. Ralf Reussner has been supportive and has given me the freedom to pursue various projects under his direction with space of my own creativity. I am grateful for his scientific advice and knowledge and many insightful discussions and suggestions, which not only shaped my dissertation but also my professional orientations. I also thank Prof. Dr. Bernhard Beckert, who was willing to act as a second referee for my thesis.

A further thank goes to my colleagues for the nice time during the last five years.

Finally, a special thank to my family and my friends.

Karlsruhe, June 2015 *Fouad ben Nasr Omri*

Contents

List of Figures

List of Tables

1. Introduction

Software reliability assessment is one of the most controversial issues in software engineering today. Software systems are omnipresent in our daily life and their failure can result in serious financial and humanitarian damages. Nevertheless, software development organizations are considering software reliability assessment as a cost rather than a return. The target of any company is to create visible benefits with least possible overhead. However, existing software reliability assessment techniques are time-consuming and labor-intensive tasks. For any realistic software system neither proof of correctness (by applying formal methods) nor existing testing and assessment techniques can guarantee failure-free software unless an unrealistic or at least impractical time and effort is taken into consideration [15]. Since proving the correctness of real software system is in most of the cases impractical to achieve, quantitative assessment of the software system reliability is usually performed. However, existing approaches for quantitative reliability assessment are controversial. Even if proof of correctness has been applied to some parts of the software, existing approaches do not formally and quantitatively account for the contribution of the confidence gained from partial proofs to the overall software reliability estimation. Consequently, software development organizations may not see direct and quantifiable return on investment when applying formal methods for reliability assessment. Furthermore, current software reliability assessment approaches, which try to be practical from the cost and overhead point of view, are usually making use of reliability prediction models based on unrealistic assumptions about the software failure process. Such assumptions result in too optimistic reliability estimate compared to real situations [62]. As a consequence, software development organizations loose their trust on such approaches and do not necessarily see the benefit of applying them. Additionally, existing software reliability assessment approaches require special knowledge, training and qualification of the software engineers involved in the reliability assessment, which makes the adoption of such approaches within a development organization a costly task. Therefore, credible and cost-effective reliability assessment techniques are urgently needed [59].

In this dissertation, we developed an automated approach for the assessment of the reliability of software systems which, compared to the existing approaches:

- reduces the cost and time required for reliability assessment given a target statistical confidence on the reliability estimate
- guarantees a return on investment for any invested testing effort: our approach guarantees that for a given test budget, the approach returns the best possible reliability estimate with the highest possible statistical confidence
- avoids possible overestimation of the reliability estimate: our approach uses theoretical sound models for reliability estimation to avoid unrealistic assumptions about the software failure process
- guarantees a return on investment when applying formal verification techniques even when partially applied to parts of the software source code: our approach integrates formal verification in the quantitative software reliability assessment, by quantitatively assessing the confidence gained from the qualitative formal verification of the source code or part of it in the reliability estimate
- reduces possible errors introduced by the software engineer when parameterizing prediction models: our approach uses non-parametric models for reliability prediction
- reduces the qualification and knowledge required from the software engineers to assess software reliability: our approach is automated and hides the mathematical and theoretical details used for assessing the reliability

1.1. Motivation

Software reliability is defined as the probability of failure-free software operation for a specified period of time and environment [4].

Software systems have become larger and more complex and our dependence on them is growing. Due to the availability of computing resources at a low cost, software systems are used in a variety of applications where their failure can result in human life and/or environmental and financial damages. Software systems are used in a common applications such as mobile phones and navigation systems; in more complex applications such as banking systems and telecommunication systems; and even in life-critical applications such as radiation systems in medicine and railway traffic control systems.

The increasing usage of software systems has resulted in an increased concern about the reliability of the software systems, which do not only concern software development organizations but also the users of such software systems. Software development organizations are concerned with the reliability of their software to face the increasing competition and in some cases to satisfy the requirements of regulatory agencies. The users are increasingly aware of the failure of software systems especially in critical applications. The media has highlighted the consequences of unreliable software such as the recent crash of the Airbus A400M in May 9, 2015 because of a software failure [1].

The fact that a software system can lead to operational failures sets a pressing need to ensure that, when a software system is used, its reliability is adequate. This means that the reliability of the software system should be assessed before using it. It must be possible either to demonstrate that the software system will execute reliably in all expected operational scenarios or to estimate the unreliability of the software system and make sure that it is adequate for the application scenario. Software reliability assessment is needed to certify software systems by regulatory agencies, or to determine the conditions of service level agreements and warranties.

The increasing complexity and the induced cost of modern software systems as well as the market competitiveness are forcing software companies to reuse existing software components whenever possible or purchase (Commercial Off-The-Shelf components, COTS) components from third-party providers. The reliability of a component-based software systems can be determined based on the reliability of the constituent components and their interaction [13]. Assessing the reliability of a component can be very important in cases of re-using the component. Furthermore, regulatory agencies usually fix reliability requirements for each component constituting a software system

[59]. Consequently, it is necessary to assess the reliability of the components used in a software system.

Therefore, the reliability assessment of a software system can be broken down into the assessment of the constituent components. Such component can be (i) black-box, i.e., the source code implementing the component is not available (e.g., purchased COTS components) or (ii) white-box, i.e., the source code is available. Different reliability assessment techniques has been proposed for the reliability assessment of black-box as well as of white-box components. In the following section, we will give an overview about these techniques and their limitations.

1.1.1. Existing Reliability Assessment Approaches: State of the Art, Challenges and Limitations

We give a high-level overview of the state-of-the-art, their limitations and the challenges related to the approach presented in this thesis. A more detailed description of related techniques is given in Chapter 7.

The novel techniques we present in this thesis are extensions as well as novel combinations of the two main approaches for the assessment of software systems reliability: deductive formal verification of source code and testing. Deductive formal verification requires the availability of the source code as well as formal specification of the functionalities implemented by the source code. Consequently, formal verification can only be used for formally specified white-box components. Testing can be used for white-box as well as black-box components [1].

1.1.1.1. Deductive Source Code Verification

Deductive source code verification is a technique to prove the correctness of a software with respect to a formal specification. The specification describes the expected behavior of the software consumed and provided methods based on pre-and post-conditions following the design-by-contract [64] and Hoare-style [53] principles. For instance, state-of-the-art deductive verification

[1] Note that testing also requires some kind of specification, e.g., test oracles.

systems include KeY [8], ESC/Java2 [24], VCC [23], as well as the proof assistants PVS [74] and Isabelle/HOL [93]. Most of these tools make use of symbolic execution or weakest precondition computation to transform the source code and the specification into first-order logic formulas called proof obligations. Proof obligation are generated by a verification tool and if theses obligations can be verified (or closed), for example using theorem provers like KeY or SMT solvers like Z3 [31] then the reliability of the software is proven, i.e., the software is reliable w.r.t the specification. The goal of the verification tools is to close all generated proof obligations.

When the software is correct with respect to its specification, then, experience shows, that verification tools can usually prove the correctness of the program automatically. Under the assumption that the specification is correct (i.e., conform to the expected behavior of the software), source code verification can be used to induce the software reliability. However, because of the semi-decidability of first-order logic, if the program contains faults, the proof search may never terminate (unless a timeout is set). In such as case the user does not know whether the program is correct or not, and usually a user interaction may be required to advance the proof. Recent techniques [41], are making use of the information provided with the open proof obligations to detect faults and generate counterexamples. However, none of the existing techniques, as far as we know, is able to quantify the software reliability in the presence of open proof obligations. Therefore, the challenge is (i) how to formally and quantitatively account for any verification effort in the reliability estimate and (ii) how can we give a statement about the software reliability when not all proof obligations are proved.

In practice, however, it is usually impractical to rigorously apply formal verification to all relevant components (e.g. compiler, hardware, network) related to the execution environment of the software. In addition, a software can use COTS components where usually the source code is not available. In such as case, verification based test cases [6, 42] are generated. The goal of testing is to reveal software faults. The benefit of formal verification in this case is to generate high coverage test cases that are strong at revealing software failures [6]. However, exhaustive testing (verification by testing) is practically impossible for complex software systems with large input domains. The challenge is then, how to avoid exhaustive testing when verification is done.

1.1.1.2. Testing based on Operational Profiles

Since exhaustive testing is usually impractical for complex real software systems with large input domains, statistical testing is proposed as a resort [57]. Statistical testing is random black-box testing where test cases are randomly drawn from the software input space according to an operational profile. The operational profile is a quantitative approximation of the software's operational use. Formally, an operational profile can be defined as $OP = \{(\mathcal{D}_i, p_i) | i \in \{1, 2, \ldots, L\}, \sum_{i=1}^{L} p_i = 1\}$ [69]. The OP is a set of pairs $(\mathcal{D}_i, p_i)$, where $\mathcal{D}_i$ represents a set of sub-domains of the global input domain $\mathcal{D}$ to describe a possible operational scenario, and p_i is the probability that an operational input belongs to $\mathcal{D}_i$. Usually, a reliability tester has reliability targets consisting of the required reliability value of the software and the required statistical confidence on the reliability estimate. Statistical testing is then applied to the software and testing stops when (i) the required reliability value cannot be reached because testing revealed failures, or (ii) the required reliability value is estimated with the target statistical confidence.

Given an operational profile, statistical testing estimates the reliability of the software using the following statistical estimator $\hat{R} = 1 - \sum_{i=1}^{L} p_i FP_i$. The crucial part of the estimation is the approximation of the failure probability FP_i when the software is executed with inputs from $\mathcal{D}_i$. Existing models to approximate FP_i can be grouped in three different categories: (i) fault seeding models, (ii) software reliability growth models and (iii) sampling models.

Fault seeding models are statistical fault injection models which make assumptions about the distribution of faults remaining in the program after testing. Such assumptions cannot be rigorously justified and the representativeness of the injected faults is questionable [79]. Software reliability growth models (SRGMs) extrapolate the future failure probability based on failure data indexed by time. Such models, however, have many shortcomings related to their unrealistic assumptions and inaccurate predictability [98]. Sampling models are theoretically sound [87], but they suffer from several practical problems. Sampling models require a large number of test cases [15] to gain high confidence on the reliability estimate.

Consequently, in order to avoid unrealistic assumptions about the software failure process, and in order to increase the trust of software reliability practitioners on the reliability estimate produced by statistical testing, sampling models have to be used. The remaining challenge is how to reduce the required number of test cases to gain a target confidence on the reliability estimate. Recently published approaches such as [92] and [37] present techniques to accelerate statistical testing based on path coverage criteria. Both techniques assume that a single test case pro program path is enough for reliability testing. They assume that repeated testing of the same program path cannot contribute to fault detection. They generate randomly only one input to execute each program path. However, we believe that their assumption can be very misleading. If a program path does not contain faults, then all inputs executing that path will execute successfully. However, when a program path contains faults, some inputs executing that path may coincidentally produce correct outputs. Consequently, a single test case selected from the program path input domain may not be able to detect the faults and this may cause an overestimation of the software reliability. An illustrative example of such faults are domain faults, which are faults in the control flow that cause wrong program paths to be executed [96]. Domain faults build shifts in the domain boundaries of the inputs executing the program path. If such shifts are small, then most of the inputs executing the faulty program path will produce correct outputs. Consequently, there is a very low probability that a single randomly generated input from the program path input domain can be the fault revealing input.

Furthermore, these approaches usually rely on bounded symbolic execution to extract the program paths. Bounded symbolic execution is used to avoid the path explosion problem, in the presence of recursive method calls and loops. The bound limits the search depth of the symbolic execution procedure. However, such a bound is user defined and is arbitrary set without any connection to the reliability estimation targets (i.e., the required reliability value of the software as well as the required confidence). The higher the bound of symbolic execution, the more program paths are explored, the higher the confidence on the reliability estimate. The challenge is how to formally define bounds for the symbolic execution which are related to the reliability estimation targets.

Another approach [27], accelerates testing by applying monotonic transformations to the software program and the execution environment (e.g., program slicing, replacing function computation by table lookup, use of fast process simulation or use of centralized instead of distributed computing). Such transformations imply the correctness of the original program, and a failure of the transformed program does not necessary means that the original program would fail. This would require the invocation and test of the original version. In addition, the approach presented in [27] is labor-intensive requiring the formal verification of each transformation by skilled software engineers, which would limit the applicability of the approach.

All the existing approaches to reduce the number of required test cases are based on source code information with the exception of one recently published approach [54], which is adapted for black-box testing and formulates testing as an optimization problem based on the gradient-descent method. In order to reduce the risk to get stuck in a local minimum when using the gradient-descent method, the approach in [54] introduces an artificial bias in the reliability estimate. Furthermore, the approach in [54] does not generate the test cases according to the distribution of the operational profile, which would additionally bias the reliability estimate. Thus, the challenge is how to reduce the number of required test cases to reach a target statistical confidence on the reliability estimate when we have no source code available and without biasing the reliability estimate as in [54].

Reliability assessment based on testing is usually suffering from the high sensitivity of the reliability estimates to variations of the operational profile. Indeed, specifying the operational profile is an erroneous and difficult task [69]. The specified probability p_i of a sub-domain $\mathcal{D}_i$ may be erroneous to some extent. In order to cope with such difficulties, the reduction of the input space was proposed in the literature as the promising solution [69]. [26] proposes reducing the input domain using vertical slicing and program transformation, which can be labor-intensive for realistic programs.

1.1.2. Software Reliability in terms of Probabilities

One can wonder why software reliability is described in terms of probabilities. Indeed, a software does not wear out or break while executing it. A software execution is deterministic, either it is fault free and will never fail or it contains faults and any inputs which execute the faults will always cause the faults. Hardware components, however, can fail randomly during execution in the same circumstances where they previously have worked failure-free.

Usually, software failures are distinguished from random hardware failures by calling them systematic failures [59]. This can be sometimes misleading suggesting that we might handle software failure deterministically. However, it should be noted that the calling software failures as systematic failures refers to the mechanism how a fault is revealed as failure and does not refer to the failure process. The term systematic, refers to the fact that if a software failures is triggered by a particular input, then the software will always fail on that input until the responsible software fault is repaired. Consequently, the term systematic should not be considered as a form of determinism.

However, a software system is embedded in a stochastic environment (i.e., the execution environment consisting of the hardware and software environment as well as the users of the software). Such an environment subjects the software program to unpredictable inputs over time. Indeed, we cannot predict with certainty all the future inputs that will execute the software. Each input can either execute an existing software fault or not. Thus, in a system context, the software system fails in a stochastic manner. The software failure process is described by the random execution of software faults by the uncertain future inputs. Such an uncertainty can only be described using the theory of probability which is the classical theory to deal with uncertainty. Describing software reliability by a probabilistic models allows us to express our uncertainty and our confidence on the reliability estimation of software systems.

Consequently, we can consider software reliability assessment as the process to resolve the uncertainty about the software future behavior and gain knowledge of it. This resembles the famous Schrödinger's cat problem [83].

1.2. Problem Statement

Formal verification can prove the correctness of an implementation with respect to a specification. However, it is usually not practical to rigorously apply formal verification to all relevant components of the execution environment. If formal verification has been applied to only the source code of the software or part of it, existing reliability assessment approaches do not quantitatively and formally account for the confidence gained from formal verification in the reliability estimation.

Statistical testing based on sampling models is theoretical sound but requires a large number of test cases to reach a target confidence on the reliability estimate. Furthermore, the reliability estimate when statistical testing is used is usually sensitive to variations in the operational profile.

In this thesis, we developed an automated software reliability assessment approach which is both theoretical sound and practical. We believe that software reliability assessment is a process to resolve the uncertainty about the future behavior of the software under study in analogy to the famous Schrödinger's cat problem [83]. We formulated our approach as an uncertainty reduction technique, which aims to use the available information about the software in order to efficiently assess and reduce the uncertainty about the software future behavior. The information can be provided from (i) previous test cases execution, (ii) the source code of the software (ii) previous formal verification attempts. Consequently, the more information we have about the software under study the more our approach gains on efficiency and the more the uncertainty about the software failure process is systematically reduced.

Furthermore, we show that our approach is able to reduce the sensitivity of the reliability estimate to variations of the operational profile based on variance reduction of the reliability estimate and systematic input domain pruning of the software.

1.3. Main Idea of the Approach

In the following we illustrate the main idea behind our approach based on two software assessment scenarios the assessment of software components with required (i) moderate reliability, and (ii) ultra-high reliability. The levels of required reliability are defined as [15]:

- Ultra-High reliability: failure rate $< 10^{-7}$
- Moderate reliability: failure rate between 10^{-3} and 10^{-7}
- Low reliability: failure rate $> 10^{-3}$

1.3.1. Moderate Reliability Assessment

Consider the following reliability assessment scenario: a regulatory agency wants to assess the reliability of a software component. The required reliability is $1 - 10^{-5}$ with a confidence level of 0.9999 (i.e., 99.99%).

Using hypothesis testing, the required number of failure-free test cases execution is computed as: $n = \lceil \frac{log(1-0.9999)}{log(1-10^{-5})} \rceil = 921030$ (derivation can be found in Section 2.2.3).

The test cases are then executed according to an expected operational profile as shown in Section 2.1.3. When the test execution terminates:

- either no failures are revealed and consequently, the software component is reliable as required
- or some failures are revealed, in such a case the reliability of the software as well as its variance is higher that expected

In the case when testing reveals failures, the responsible faults should be repaired and 921030 new test cases are executed. Consequently, the problem causing the huge number of test cases in the case of assessing moderate reliable software, arises when failures are revealed during testing.

Existing approaches would start new testing after repairing software faults, without taking into consideration the previous effort invested in testing and the distribution of the revealed failures across the operational profile sub-domains. However, such information is very valuable. Sub-domains where no failures are revealed should not receive the same importance as the ones where failures are revealed. The intensity of the failures in each sub-domain should be an indicator of where testing should be focused. Our approach makes use of the information provided by previous test runs, to optimally allocate future test cases across the operational sub-domains in order to reduce the required number of test cases to reach a target confidence on the reliability estimate.

1.3.2. Ultra-High Reliability Assessment

Now, let's consider the case of assessing ultra-high reliable software components. Assume that the required reliability is $1 - 10^{-9}$ with a confidence of at least 99.99%. This would require the execution of $9,210,340,628$ failure-free test cases. If we assume that we can execute 10 test cases per second, this would mean that a total of $10,660$ days of testing are required. This is obviously impossible to realize.

In the case of ultra-high reliable software, we assume that some effort of formal verification has been done during the development of such software. Even, if the formal verification of such a software has been done only to some parts of it, it would delivers us some confidence that such parts will execute failure-free. Our approach proposes a method to quantitatively account for the confidence gained from applying formal verification. We use such information to systematically reduce the required number of test cases execution.

Even if a formal verification attempt terminates without closing all proof obligations as illustrated in 1.1.1.1, we believe that we can benefit from it as follows. Closed proof branches should make us more confident that parts of the software will perform correctly. On the other side, open proof branches should reduce the user confidence on the software reliability.

We present a novel approach to quantitatively assess the contribution of the closed proof obligations to the software reliability and the contribution of the open proof obligations to the confidence (or uncertainty) about the software reliability. The approach we present is able to make a quantitative statement about the software reliability even when the proof attempt fails.

1.4. Contributions

The contributions of this thesis can be arranged in three groups:

Black-box Reliability Assessment: we developed an adaptive black-box reliability assessment approach based on sampling models. The approach learns from previous test cases executions and computes in an iterative manner the required number of test cases to be executed based on user required confidence level. The approach, compared to state-of-the-art approaches, reduces the required number of test cases to reach a target statistical confidence on the reliability estimate. Furthermore, the approach allows to predict the failure rate for future test cases executions based on a non-parametric reliability model. This allows to reduce the overhead of testing. The prediction model makes effective use of previous test executions during model inference. Based on the uncertainty on the prediction and confidence goals on the reliability estimate, the approach decides whether to execute the test cases or not.

White-box Reliability Assessment: If in addition to the operational profile, the source code if available, our approach benefits from the white-box information available to further enhance the efficiency of the black-box approach. We developed an automated probabilistic analysis approach of source code based on symbolic execution. The white-box approach propagates the uncertain information provided by the operational profile while executing the source code symbolically. Compared to the black-box approach, the white-box approach makes use of the source code information to further reduce the number of required test cases to reach a target statistical confidence on the reliability estimate. More importantly, we show that the white-box approach is able to systematically reduce the sensitivity of variations of the operational profile on the reliability estimate.

Verification-Based Reliability Assessment: Traditionally, formal verification techniques and statistical testing were studied in separate research communities. However, when used separately, none of them is sufficiently powerful and practical to provide high confidence in reliability assessment. If in addition to the source code, a formal specification of the software component is also available, we propose a software reliability assessment approach which combines the strengths of formal verification and statistical testing in a unified and coherent form. The reliability estimate is derived from the proof tree. If the reliability goal cannot be reached by symbolic computation of the reliability, the approach complements the reliability estimate by test cases derived from the open proof branches. The test cases are derived using the white-box reliability assessment approach. The developed approach analyzes the reliability of a program in a runtime environment without explicitly modeling the environment in the verification logic.

1.5. Outline

This dissertation is structured as follows: In Chapter 2, we will present the foundations and current practices related to our approach. The first contribution of this dissertation will be the black-box reliability assessment approach, which is presented in Chapter 3. The concepts of the white-box reliability assessment approach are described in Chapter 4. Chapter 5, describes the verification-based reliability assessment approach, and related work is discussed in Chapter 7. We will discuss case studies for the validation of our approach in Chapter 6. The thesis closes with a look at future work the conclusion in Chapter 8.

2. Foundations and Current Practices

2.1. Software Reliability Assessment

This section presents basic definition and principles related to software reliability assessment.

2.1.1. Software Reliability Definition and Key Concepts

Software reliability is defined by ANSI/IEEE standards as "the probability of failure-free operation of a software in a specified environment for a specified time" [4]. Here, we should differentiate between the *software implementation* or the *program*, and the *software system* or shortly the *software*, which consists of the program as well as the execution environment. In the context of reliability assessment, the subject of study is the program together with its execution environment (i.e., software system), since software reliability is assessed when the program is executed or in operation.

Software unlike hardware do not wear out. Software failures are caused by faults that are present at the beginning of the software lifetime. The presence of such faults can cause the software to fail occasionally. Hence, it is useful, and sometimes because of regulatory issues necessary, to estimate the likelihood of a software failure.

Usually a program behaves deterministically. Consequently, a software failure is not a random process. However, when the program is executed in a concrete runtime environment it will be subject to stochastic random events which can compromise the correct execution. For each event, the program either operates failure-free or not. Such stochastic random events are produced by the user inputs to the software. The user inputs are usually specified with some uncertainty, and probability theory is the calculus of reasoning with uncertainty. In fact, assumptions about the inputs which will be supplied to the software are usually modeled as a stochastic process to describe such uncertainty. Consequently, software reliability is defined as the probability that an input supplied to the software would lead to a failure-free execution of the software.

It may be argued that it should be possible to deterministically detect which inputs to the software would lead to a failure. This can be achieved by proving the correctness of the implementation and the execution environment with respect to a specification using formal verification techniques. However, it is usually not practical to rigorously apply formal verification to all relevant components (e.g. compiler, hardware, network) related to the execution environment of the program. Another possible solution to the reliability problem would be to test all admissible inputs of the software. However, this would generally not be possible since the number of admissible inputs is usually prohibitively large for real world programs. As an illustration, consider the portion of code in Listing 2.1. The `FLAG` array will generate $2^{100} = 1.2676506 \times 10^{30}$ possible inputs and testing all of them will be very challenging.

Consequently, software reliability is not a quality of the software alone but a function of the software's quality together with the way how the software is used. therefore, it does not make sense to talk about software reliability estimate without associating the estimate with assumptions about how the software will be used.

In the following section, we describe how such assumptions are formulated in form of *operational profiles* which quantify the likelihood that an input is supplied to the software.

2.1.2. Operational Profile

The idea of an operational profile and its relation to the reliability estimate can be illustrated by the following standard example taken from [85]. Consider we have a program which uses a stack data structure with the three operations (i) `PUSH(a)`, which puts the value a on top of the stack, (ii) `POP()`, which removes the value on the top of the stack and (iii) `TOP()`, which returns the value on the top of the stack.

Suppose that the implementation of the operation `TOP()` contains the following fault: two successive calls to the operation `TOP()` will return different values, with the second one being wrong.

Now if we would test the three operations randomly with the assumption that all operations are equally likely to be invoked, we would then get a low reliability estimate for the studied program. However, it is generally rare to call the operation `TOP()` twice successively because the user knows that `TOP()` does not change the top value of the stack. Additionally, the probability to call the operation `TOP()` after calling `PUSH(a)` is very low, because the caller knows that the actual top value of the stack is the value a just put on top of the stack. If we would test the program with a probability distribution that reflects such facts, we expect the reliability of the program under study to be high because the situations which would execute the fault in the operation `TOP()` would rarely arise.

```
if(FLAG[0] == false) {
  M0();
}
if(FLAG[1] == false) {
  M1();
}
if(FLAG[2] == false) {
  M2();
}
if(FLAG[3] == false) {
  M3();
}
.
.
.
if(FLAG[100] == false) {
  M100();
}
```

Listing 2.1: A sample portion of code

Consequently, in order to make a software reliability assessment which is relevant to the expected users of the software, the software should be tested while taking into account the patterns of usage specific to the expected users. The way how the users interact with the software is usually a non-deterministic process. Therefore, probabilistic models are used to describe the interaction of the users with the software. Such patterns are quantitatively captured by the operation profile specific to the expected users.

The operational profile is composed by two parts:

- the set of all possible executions of the software, to be denoted by $\mathcal{E}$
- a probability distribution over $\mathcal{E}$

Following [85], $\mathcal{E}$ describes all sequences of executions the user can perform on the software:

$$\mathcal{E} = \{\mathcal{EV}_i, \mathcal{EV}_j, \mathcal{EV}_i\mathcal{EV}_j, \mathcal{EV}_i\mathcal{EV}_j\mathcal{EV}_k, \ldots\}$$

Each execution consists of one or more events $\mathcal{EV}$. Each event consists of one or more method or operation calls which are implemented by the software under study. Each execution is also assigned a probability which indicate the frequencies with which the user would issue the execution.

For each execution $\mathcal{I}_i \in \mathcal{E}$, the corresponding probability is denoted by $\mathbb{P}(\mathcal{I}_i)$. In order to have a proper probability distribution, the following two conditions should hold:

- $0 \leq \mathbb{P}(\mathcal{I}_i) \leq 1 \; \forall \mathcal{I}_i \in \mathcal{E}$
- $\sum_{\mathcal{I}_i \in \mathcal{E}} \mathbb{P}(\mathcal{I}_i) = 1$

An input oriented presentation of the operational profile, as proposed by [69], is to represent each execution $\mathcal{I}_i$ with the possible inputs that would lead to its execution. Assume that the operational profile describes L possible executions and that the input domain of the software under study is denoted by $\mathcal{D}$. Following [69], the operational profile divides then the input domain $\mathcal{D}$ of the software to test in L sub-domains: $\mathcal{D}_1, \mathcal{D}_2, \ldots, \mathcal{D}_L$. Each sub-domain represents a possible operational use or a possible execution of the software and has a probability of occurrence according the operational profile. Let p_i be the probability of occurrence of sub-domain $\mathcal{D}_i$. The OP can therefore represented as $OP = \{(\mathcal{D}_i, p_i) | i = \{1, 2, \ldots, L\}, \sum_{i=1}^{L} p_i = 1\}$.

2.1.3. Statistical Testing

Statistical testing is a special form of random testing where test cases are selected based on the input distributions specified by a given operational profile. Statistical testing is a treatment of the software testing process as a statistical inference task. In such a statistical inference task, the input domain $\mathcal{D}$ as specified by the operational profile is the population of study, the sub-domains $\mathcal{D}_i$ are the strata, the test cases are the samples and the probability p_i of sub-domain $\mathcal{D}_i$ is the sampling distribution. The inference is then the process of estimating the reliability of the software when executed with inputs from the population based on the distribution specified by the operational profile.

Statistical Testing as proposed by Musa [69] generates by random sampling test cases according to the operational profile.

Let $\mathcal{A}$ a sequence defined as follows: $\mathcal{A} = \{\mathcal{A}_0, \mathcal{A}_1, \ldots, \mathcal{A}_L\}$, $|\mathcal{A}| = L + 1$, where $\mathcal{A}_i = \sum_{k=1}^{i} p_i$ for $i = 1, \ldots, L$, and $\mathcal{A}_0 = 0$.

The generation of the test cases is then as follows:

1. Generate a uniformly distributed random number $\zeta \in (0, 1)$, if $\zeta \in [\mathcal{A}_i, \mathcal{A}_{i+1}]$, then the sub-domain $\mathcal{D}_{i+1}$ will be randomly sampled since $\mathcal{A}_{i+1} - \mathcal{A}_i = p_{i+1}$, where p_{i+1} the probability of occurrence of sub-domain $\mathcal{D}_{i+1}$.

2. Generate input variables from the sub-domain $\mathcal{D}_{i+1}$ based on the provided input distributions, and execute the test case.

3. Repeat the above steps until a stopping criteria is reached (e.g, target reliability value reached, target confidence on the estimated reliability reached, required test time reached, etc,...)

The test selection approach proposed by Musa [69] is based on proportional stratified sampling. The selection is controlled by the uniformly distributed random variable $\zeta \in (0, 1)$.

Since testing cannot guarantee the absence of faults, exposing the software to the inputs expected to be the most frequently used should detect the failures most likely to appear during operational use. The outcome of testing is used to estimate the reliability of the software system. Statistical testing as an inference task requires the definition of a statistical estimator which will be used to estimate the population statistic which is the software reliability in our case. The software reliability estimate is modeled as a random variable and a statistical estimator is defined to approximate the reliability estimate. Given the operational profile $OP = \{(\mathcal{D}_i, p_i) | i = \{1, 2, \ldots, L\}, \sum_{i=1}^{L} p_i = 1\}$, the reliability can be estimated through the following general statistical estimator $\hat{R} = 1 - \sum_{i=1}^{L} p_i FP_i$, where $\hat{R}$ is a random variable representing the reliability estimate and FP_i is a random variable representing the failure probability of the software when executed with inputs from the sub-domain $\mathcal{D}_i$. The variance of the statistical estimator defines the statistical confidence on the computed estimate. Greater levels of variance yield larger confidence intervals, and hence less precise estimates of the software reliability.

Consequently, the goal of statistical testing as a statistical inference task is to make a precise inference about the failure probability of the software which will be used to quantify the software reliability.

In the following sections we will introduce different current practices and approaches for the estimation of the failure probability of software based on testing.

2.2. Software Reliability Models

In the following subsections we present different approaches to quantify the failure rate of software in order to estimate its reliability.

2.2.1. Software Reliability Growth Models

Software reliability growth models are time-based reliability models because they aim at predicting the evolution of the software reliability in the future. Software reliability growth models use failure data obtained after testing or operational use to extrapolate the future failure rate of the software.

A software reliability growth model is usually build in three steps. The first step is to select the mathematical model structure based on preliminary assumptions about the software system characteristics and the testing environment. Such models are usually parametric regression models. The second step is to parameterize the model by fitting the available failure data to the model. The last step is to deduce rules for the fitted model to be used to predict the future failure rate of the software under study.

Generally, software reliability growth models can be grouped in two categories: (i) time between failure models and (ii) failure count models.

2.2.1.1. Time Between Failure models

Our investigation in this model class will include the time as variable which occurs between failures. T_i is a random variable specified as time between the $(i-1)$st and the ith failures. Let us assume that T_i convert to a known distribution and its parameters depends on the amount of errors remaining in the program after the $(i-1)$st failure. The observation of the time between failures during the testing phase will give us those parameters. The fitted model can then be used to estimate the software reliability, mean time to failure, etc. [43] The most known model in this study is the Jelinski/Moranda (JM) De-eutrophication Model ([38]). According to the JM model $t_1, t_2, \ldots$ are independent and random variables that have exponential probability density functions and is described through the following equation:

$$P(t_i/z(t_i)) = z(t_i)e^{-z(t_i)t_i)}, t_i > 0 \tag{2.1}$$

$z(t_i)$ is defined as the failure rate at time t_i and t_i stand for the time between the $(i-1)$st and the ith failures:

$$z(t_i) = \Phi[N - (i-1)], \tag{2.2}$$

Φ and N are both model parameters. Φ is a proportional constant and N is the total number of faults that exists originally in the program.

Those several faults depends on each other and the probability causing a system breakdown is the same. To avoid this from happening a fault is detected and deleted in each intervals between the $(i-1)$st and ith failures so that no new faults occurs.

Both models parameters N and Φ can be estimated using the maximum likelihood method. If $t_1, , t_2, ..t_{i-1}$ are the observed data, then we can predict the reliability through the following equation:

$$\hat{R}_i(t) = e^{-(\hat{N}-(i-1)\hat{\Phi})} \tag{2.3}$$

$\hat{R}_i(t)$ is a predication of $R_i(t) = P(t_i < t)$.

The problem of using this model is the ideal debugging process and that all faults create the same failure rate.

There are also other models that works on the basics of the JM model but with some extensions and small modification. For instance the Schick/Wolverton model [82] is basically the same as the JM model except that the failure rate function depend on the current fault content of the program and the time elapsed since the last failure:

$$z(t_i) = \Phi[N - (i-1)]t_i \tag{2.4}$$

Another revised model based on the JM model is the Goel/Okumoto imperfect debugging model [45]. The Goel/Okumoto model treats the amount of faults occurring in this system at time t, $X(t)$ through the Markov process. The software here has the ability to change its own failure randomly and conduct its transition probability by imperfect debugging. In this process the time $X(t)$ is assumed to be distributed exponentially, where its rates depends on the amount of the fault content in the system. Such a failure can be described through the following function:

$$z(t_i) = [N - p(i-1)]\lambda \tag{2.5}$$

where (p) the probability of imperfect debugging and λ is the failure rate per fault.

Another model which approaches the problem differently to the JM model is the Littlewood/Verrall Bayesian Model [60]. The time between the failures in this model is exponentially distributed. The main difference here lies in the distribution $z(t_i)$ which is a random variable and depends on a gamma distribution and given by the following relationship:

$$f(z(t_i)|\alpha, \Psi(i)) = \frac{[\Psi(i)]^{\alpha} z(t_i)^{\alpha-1} e^{-\Psi(i)z(t_i)}}{\Gamma\alpha} \tag{2.6}$$

where α and $\Psi(i)$ are model parameters.

2.2.1.2. Failure Count Models

The failure count models investigate the variable which is the number of failures detected during the testing intervals. We consider in this models the time intervals to be fixed and the failures or faults between the intervals as random variable which are independent and have Poisson distribution.

The Goel/Okumoto Nonhomogenous Poisson Process (NHPP) Model [46] is one of the earliest and simplest Poisson model. The model assumes that software is subject to failures at random times caused by faults present in the system. Let $N(t)$ be the number of failures monitored at any given time t. This model describes $N(t)$ as a nonhomogeneous Poisson process with a failure rate that depends on time:

$$P(N(t) = y) = \frac{(m(t))^y}{y!} e^{-m(t)}, y = 0, 1, 2, \ldots \tag{2.7}$$

where $m(t)$ is the mean value function and gives the expected number of failures monitored by time t as:

$$m(t) = a(1 - e^{-bt}) \tag{2.8}$$

The following mathematical equation describes the failure rate:

$$z(t) \equiv m'(t) = abe^{-bt} \tag{2.9}$$

where a describes the number of failures that can be observed and b the occurrence rate of an individual fault.

This model is identical to the JM model. It assume a direct proportionality between the failure rates and the number of remaining fault. However the difference lies in the modeling process which is continuously and not discrete. The model permits imperfect debugging in which the new faults are introduced during the debugging process.

The experiments shows that the failure rate first increase and then decreases. To describe this behavior, Goel [44] proposed a generalization of Goel/Okumoto Nonhomogeneous Poisson Process Model. The model uses the mean value function form:

$$m(t) = a(1 - e^{-bt}) \tag{2.10}$$

where a is the same parameter as in the Goel/Okumoto Nonhomogeneous Model and b, c are constants that describe the quality of testing. In this case the failure rate function $z(t)$ is described as follows:

$$z(t) \equiv m'(t) = abce^{-bt}t^{c-t} \tag{2.11}$$

According to the equation, a delay exists between the fault detection and the fault removal. So the testing consist of two phases. The first phase is fault detection and the second phase is fault removal. S-shaped NHPP model is supposed to reflect this proposal([71], [47]). The mean value function $m(t)$ is described through the following relationship

$$m(t) = a(1 - (1 + bt)e^{-bt}) \tag{2.12}$$

a, b are the same parameter from the NHHP model. The failure rate is represented through the following equation:

$$z(t) \equiv m'(t) = b^2te^{-bt} \tag{2.13}$$

2.2.1.3. Limitations and Advantages of Software Reliability Growth Models

The advantage in such a software is modeling any kind of behavior during the test phase by choosing the right an appropriate model. Thus, they are easy to implement, applied and automated on all kinds of software from the simple ones to the most complex modules such as a flight control system. However, the growth models also have some limitations. First, the assumption that all the faults resulting in a software crash are probably equal. This assumption is however unrealistic because the probability that the faults appear may vary significantly. Another problem is that the capacity of the model depends on an operational profile which is considered to be available and thus all the testings runs on it. However, the profile may have big errors and changes in the operational profile which will may not produce good results. Many research has been done to analyze the sensitivity of the model predictions to error ([25], [18]). Also the predictions of the growth models are not very accurate.

We can summarize that expanded models treat the software as a black box and it doesn't take the architecture of the target software into consideration. We have also seen that there are many kinds of expanded models which have different assumption methods are used to catch the different target system architecture and their testing processes. Though some experiments have shown that such methods are not reliable and trustworthy enough to be used.

2.2.2. Fault Seeding Models

The base knowledge in this class is to implement known faults in a program that contains already a various amounts of unknown native faults. After seeding the faults in the program, the system will be tested and after that the implemented and native faults are recorded. According to the recorded data a prediction is made to estimate the software reliability.

Some models in this class include the Lipow Model and the Basin Model are economical and easy to implement. However, they are build upon an assumption that the implemented and seeded faults don't depend on each other and both have the same probability to be detected. Another disadvantage of such a model is the unreliability to find and calculate the failure rate function. Thus this limits the usage of such a model.

2.2.3. Sampling Models

The stack of all relevant inputs of a program is known as an input domain. The input domain itself exists through several input sub domain and it is uniform only if all its member causes together the system to fail or succeed. So this means in other words that every member is equally important and represent the whole sub domain. The path describes the path in a program through its sub domain.

The idea behind this model is to indicate specific amount of test cases from the input domain which represent the operation of the program. Thus the program reliability can be predicted from monitoring the failures during the execution of the test cases. The input distribution is often impossible to achieve, to simplify this complexity we split the input domain into sub domain and run the test in those layers upon a uniform distribution. be An estimate of the program reliability is obtained from the failures observed during the execution of the test cases. Since the input distribution is very difficult to obtain, the input domain is often divided into sub domains and test cases are generated randomly in each sub domain based upon a uniform distribution. There are two kinds of testing: random testing and sub domain/partition testing.

2.2.3.1. Random Testing

This random testing method select multiple test cases from the whole input domain. The oldest model that describes the Random Testing is the Nelson Model. A program P can be defined through the input domain D and it is size is given as d (> 0). We describe m ($0 \leqslant m \leqslant d$) as the number of failure-causing inputs that produce incorrect output in D. In this way the failure rate of the program, θ, can be described as follows:

$$\theta = \frac{m}{d} \tag{2.14}$$

The total number of inputs selected for testing is defined as n which is the number of failure monitored during the execution process on the inputs. θ is estimated through the following mathematical relationship:

$$\hat{\theta} = \frac{n_e}{n} \tag{2.15}$$

We assume that the program is being tested for along time using certain input distribution, this will increase the failure rate of a program to the probability that it will fail to execute upon the chosen input distribution. Therefore an equitable estimation of the software reliability per execution $\hat{R}$is described as follows:

$$\hat{R} = 1 - \hat{\theta} = 1 - \frac{n_e}{n} \tag{2.16}$$

To evaluate the strength of the random testing principal in comparison to other testing methods, we define P_r as the probability of finding at least one error in n tests.

$$P_r = 1 - (1 - \theta)^n \tag{2.17}$$

2.2.3.2. Subdomain/Partition Testing

Both testing classes (sub domain testing and partition testing) splits the input domain into sub domains. So that different test cases can be selected from each sub domain to test the program. We use the description sub domain testing when the sub domains may or may not be separated. However in comparison the term partition testing is used if all sub domains are disjoint ([20]).

The partition testing method is used to separate the input domain and select at least one test case from each sub domain. Let us partition the domain D in k sub domains and are described by D_{i},, where $i = 1, 2, ..k$. Each sub domain D_i is characterized by d_i and the failure inputs m, $(0 \leqslant m_i \leqslant d_i)$. Now we can describe the failure rate as follows:

$$\theta_i = \frac{m_i}{d_i} \tag{2.18}$$

By describing p_i as a probability in which the random selected input comes from the sub domain D_i, the failure rate of the whole program can be interrupted through the following equation:

$$\theta = \sum_{i=1}^{k} p_i \theta_i \tag{2.19}$$

n_i ($\geqslant 1$) denote the number of test cases and n_{ei} denote the number of test cases selected from the subdomain D_i which result in program failures. All the random selections are also assumed to be independent, with replacement, and based upon a uniform distribution. This means that when a test case is selected from D_i, the probability will be exactly θ_i. Using equation (2.15) we can obtain an estimate of the overall failure rate of the program. Another estimate of θ is given as follow:

$$\hat{\theta}_2 = \sum_{i=1} p_i \hat{\theta}_i = \sum_{i=1}^{k} p_i (\frac{n_{ei}}{n_i}) \tag{2.20}$$

To estimate software reliability the equation equation (2.16) can be used.

The probability of finding at least one error in n tests is P_p:

$$P_p = 1 - \prod_{i=1}^{k} (1 - \theta_i)^{n_i} \tag{2.21}$$

2.2.3.3. Discussion

Input domain sampling models unlike reliability growth models do not depend upon unrealistic assumptions such as the assumption that all the failures have the same contribution to the unreliability of the software. Sampling models implicitly weigh the contribution of each failure rate of each sub-domain to the unreliability based on the probabilities p_i of the sub-domains.

2.2.4. Palladio Component Model for Reliability Assessment

The reliability of a full PCM instance is be predicted in terms of the probability of successful execution $PSE = 1 - POFOD$ (Probability of Failure on Demands). The prediction part starts with a PCM instance as input and outputs a system reliability value. The process requires in between solving parameters dependencies. It turns all parameters in the model into their system-usage implied probability distributions, and joins possible sources of failure into an analytical approach which quantify system-level reliability [13].

A system failure may occur if an unavailable hardware is accessed during its unavailability state. In PCM, system deployers annotate hardware resources with Mean Time To Failure ($MTTF$) and Mean Time To Repair ($MTTR$) values.

2.2.4.1. Solving Parameter Dependencies

We reuse the existing PCM Dependency Solver to solve all the parameter dependencies across a PCM instance. The behavior of each software component in PCM is abstractly modeled by so-called SEFFs (Service Effect Specification). SEFFs may contain parameter dependencies that reflect the influence of input parameter values on the control and data flow. The Dependency Solver traverses recursively the specified SEFFs and resolves all parameter dependencies in its way. The dependency solver is only able to solve linear parameter dependencies. For the case of non-linear parameter dependencies, we use Monte-Carlo Integration to approximate such dependencies by simulation.

2.2.4.2. Determining Probabilities of Physical System State

The next step after solving the parameters dependencies is determining every possible physical system states and their probability of occurrence. The physical system state is built through all individual states of the system's hardware resources. Those are defined in the PCM resource environment and allocated to resource containers.
We define $R = r_1, r_2, ..., r_n$ the set of resources in the system. Each resource r_i is defined by its $MTTR_i$ and $MTTF_i$ and has two possible states OK and NA. For the reliability prediction we are not going to use in our approach the specified $MTTR_i$ and $MTTF_i$ values directly. Therefore, we calculate the steady-state availability Av of resource r_i:

$$Av(r_i) = MTTF_i/(MTTR_i + MTTF_i)$$

So $Av(r_i)$ can be interpreted as a probability that the resource is available when required through an internal action during service execution. We set t as an arbitrary point in time and $s(r_i, t)$ the state for the resource r_i at time t. Consequently, we have:

$$P(s(q_i, t) = OK) = Av(q_i)$$

$$P(s(q_i, t) = NA) = 1 - Av(q_i)$$

This equation ignores the arbitrary point in time t and act as if the system is in its steady-state. We will go further and define S that includes a set of possible physical system states, where each state $s_j \in S$ is a combination of possible states for all n resources at time t.

$$s_j = (s_j(r_1, t), s_j(r_2, t)..., s_j(r_n, t)) \in \{OK, NA\}^n$$

As each resource has two states *OK* and *NA*, there are 2^n physical system state. Let $P(s_j, t)$ be the probability of a system that can exist in a state s_j at time t. The probability of each physical system state is the product of the individual resource-state probabilities

$$\forall j \in \{1, ..., m\} : P(s_j, t) = \prod_{i=1}^{n} P(s(r_i, t) = s_j(r_i, t))$$

2.2.4.3. Generating and Evaluating the Markov Model

In order to predict the reliably of a system in a recursive way, we have to generate and evaluate the Discrete-Time Markov Chains. (DTMCs). DTMCs is based on PCM dependencies parameter solver and a known physical system state with probability of happening. The DTMCs algorithm consist of two section. The first section is generation and evaluation which exist in a physical system state. In the second section the final result is obtained through gathering all the individual results. The behavioral action of the PCM instance are continually transformed into Markov chains as shown in figure section 2.2.4.3.

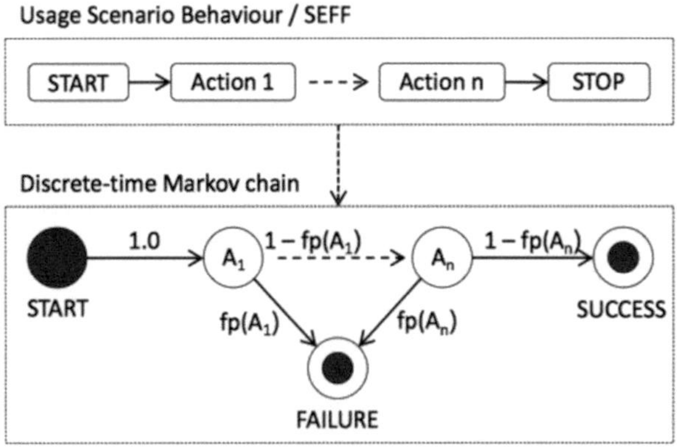

Figure 2.1.: Markov chain generation [13]

2.3. Statistical Inference and Sampling

Mathematical statistics is the science of dealing with uncertain phenomenon and events. Two basic concepts of statistics are population and sample. The definitions in this section are taken from [40] and [97].

Definition 2.1. *Population is the collection of all individuals or items under consideration in a statistical study.*

The features of the population under investigation can be usually summarized by numerical parameters.

Definition 2.2. *Sample is that part of the population from which information is collected.*

Definition 2.3. *A probability space over a finite set is a triple* $(\Omega, \mathcal{F}, P)$ *consisting of*

1. *a sample space* Ω *which is a non-empty finite set,*
2. *the set F of all subsets of* Ω*,*
3. *a probability measure on* $(\Omega, \mathcal{F})$*, that is, a map* $P : \mathcal{F} \rightarrow \mathcal{R}$ *which is*
    - *positive:* $P(A) \geq 0$ *for all* $A \in \mathcal{F}$*,*
    - *normed:* $P(\Omega) = 1$*, and*
    - *additive: if* $A_1, A_2, ..., A_n \in \mathcal{F}$ *are mutually disjoint, then*

    $$P(\bigcup_{i=1}^{n} A_i) = \sum_{i=1}^{n} P(A_i)$$

    The elements of Ω *are called outcomes, the elements of* $\mathcal{F}$ *are called events.*

Definition 2.4. *For any events A and B of the probability space* $(\Omega, \mathcal{F}, P)$ *we have*

1. $P(A) + P(A_c) = 1.$
2. $P(\varnothing) = 0.$

3. *if* $A \subseteq B$*,then* $P(B\ A) = P(B) - P(A)$*and hence* $P(A) \leq P(B)$ *(and so P is increasing).*

4. $P(A \cup B) = P(A) + P(B) - P(A \cap B)$.

Point distribution

Definition 2.5. *Let* $(\Omega, \mathcal{F}, P)$ *be a probability space over a finite set* Ω*. The function*

$$\begin{aligned} P : \Omega &\longrightarrow [0; 1] \\ \omega &\mapsto P(\omega) \end{aligned}$$

is the point probability function (or the probability mass function) of $\mathcal{P}$*. Point probabilities are often visualized as "probability bars".*

Definition 2.6. *Let* $(\Omega, \mathcal{F}, P)$ *be a probability space, let A and B be events, and suppose that* $P(B) > 0$*. The number*

$$P(A|B) = \frac{P(A \cap B)}{P(B)}$$

is called the conditional probability of A given B.

Definition 2.7. *Let* $(\Omega, \mathcal{F}, P)$ *be a probability space, let A and B be events, and suppose that* $P(B) > 0$*. The function*

$$\begin{aligned} P(.|B) : \mathcal{F} &\longrightarrow [0; 1] \\ A &\mapsto P(A|B) \end{aligned}$$

is called the conditional distribution given B.

Bayes' formula: shows how to calculate the posterior probabilities $P(B_j|A)$ from the prior probabilities $P(B_j)$ and the conditional probabilities $P(A|B_j)$.

Definition 2.8. *Let* $A = \cup_{i=1}^{k} A \cap B_i$ *where the sets* $A \cap B_i$ *are disjoint, we have*

$$P(A) = \sum_{i=1}^{k} P(A \cap B_i) = \sum_{i=1}^{k} P(A|B_i)P(B_i)$$

and since $P(B_j|A) = P(A \cap B_j)/P(A) = P(A|B_j)P(B_j)/P(A)$*,we obtain*

$$P(B_j|A) = \frac{P(A|B_j)P(B_j)}{\sum_{i=1}^{k} P(A|B_i)P(B_i)}$$

Definition 2.9. *The events* $A_1, A_2, ..., A_k$ *are said to be independent, if it is true that for any subset* $A_{i_1}, A_{i_2}, ..., A_{i_m}$ *of these events,*

$$P(\bigcap_{j=1}^{m} A_{i_j}) = \prod_{j=1}^{m} P(A_{i_j})$$

Random Variable: random variables are most frequently denoted by capital letters (such as X, Y, Z).

Definition 2.10. *Let* $(\Omega, \mathcal{F}, P)$ *be a probability space over a finite set. A random variable* $((\Omega, \mathcal{F}, P)$ *is a map* X *from* Ω *to* $\mathcal{R}$*, the set of reals. More general, an n-dimensional random variable on* $(\Omega, \mathcal{F}, P)$ *is a map* X *from* Ω *to* $\mathcal{R}^{\setminus}$.

Distribution Function

Definition 2.11. *The distribution function* F *of a random variable* X *is the function*

$$F \longrightarrow [0; 1]$$

$$x \longmapsto P(X \leqslant x)$$

A distribution function has certain properties:

Definition 2.12. *If the random variable* X *has distribution function* F*, then*

$$P(X \leqslant x) = F(x)$$

$$P(X > x) = 1 - F(x)$$

$$P(a < X \leqslant b) = F(b) - F(a)$$

for any real numbers x *and* $a < b$.

The distribution function is not the best way to give an informative visualisation of the distribution of a random variable. The *probability function* is a far better tool. The probability function for the random variable X is considered as a function defined on the range of X:

$$f : x \mapsto P(X = x)$$

Definition 2.13. *The probability function of a random variable X is the function*

$$f : x \mapsto P(X = x)$$

Definition 2.14. *For a given distribution the distribution function F and the probability function f are related as follows:*

$$f(x) = F(x) - F(x-)$$

$$F(x) = \sum_{z:z \leq x} f(z)$$

Independent random variables Let $X_1, X_2, ..., X_n$ be random variables on the same finite probability space. Their joint probability function is the function

$$f(x_1, x_2, ..., x_n) = P(X_1 = x_1, X_2 = x_2, ..., X_n = x_n).$$

For each j the function

$$f_j(x_j) = P(X_j = x_j)$$

is called the marginal probability function of X_j. If we have a non-trivial set of indices $i_1, i_2, ..., i_k \subset 1, 2, ..., n$, then

$$f_{i_1, i_2, ..., i_k}(x_{i_1}, x_{i_2}, ..., x_{i_k}) = P(X_{i_1} = x_{i_1}, X_{i_2} = x_{i_2}, ..., X_{i_k} = x_{i_k})$$

is the marginal probability function of $X_{i_1}, X_{i_2}, ..., X_{i_k}$. The independence of random variables:

Definition 2.15. *Let $(\Omega, \mathcal{F}, P)$ be a probability space over a finite set. Then the random variables $X_1, X_2, ..., X_n$ on $(\Omega, \mathcal{F}, P)$ are said to be independent, if for any choice of subsets $B_1, B_2, ..., B_n$ of $\mathcal{R}$, the events $X_1 \in B_1$, $X_2 \in B_2$,..., $X_n \in B_n$ are independent.*

Definition 2.16. *The random variables $X_1, X_2, ..., X_n$ are independent, if and only if*

$$P(X_1 = x_1, X_2 = x_2, ..., X_n = x_n) = \prod_{i=1}^{n} P(X_i = x_i)$$

for all n-tuples $x_1, x_2, ..., x_n$ of real numbers such that x_i belongs to the range of X_i, $i = 1, 2, ..., n$.

Definition 2.17. *The random variables $X_1, X_2, ..., X_n$ are independent, if and only if their joint probability function equals the product of the marginal probability functions:*

$$f_{12...n}(x_1, x_2, ..., x_n) = f_1(x_1)f_2(x_2)...f_n(x_n).$$

Expectation The expectation or mean value of a real-valued function is a weighted average of the values that the function takes.

Definition 2.18. *The expectation, or expected value, or mean value, of a real random variable X on a finite probability space $(\Omega, \mathcal{F}, P)$ is the real number*

$$E(x) = \sum_{\omega \in \Omega} X(\omega)P(\omega)$$

Definition 2.19. *If X and Y are independent random variables on the probability space $(\Omega, \mathcal{F}, P)$, then $E(XY) = E(X)E(Y)$.*

Definition 2.20. *If A is an event and $\mathbf{1}_A$ its indicator function, then $E(\mathbf{1}_A) = P(A)$.*

Variance and covariance

Definition 2.21. *The variance of the random variable X is the real number*

$$Var(X) = E\left((X - EX)^2\right) = E(X^2) - (EX)^2.$$

The standard deviation of X is the real number $\sqrt{Var(X)}$

Definition 2.22. *The covariance between two random variables X and Y on the same probability space is the real number*

$$Cov(X,Y) = E\left((X - EX)(Y - EY)\right).$$

The following rules are easily shown:

Definition 2.23. *For any random variables X, Y, U, V and any real numbers a, b, c, d*

$$\begin{aligned} Cov(X,X) &= Var(X) \\ Cov(X,Y) &= Cov(Y,X) \\ Cov(X,a) &= 0 \\ Cov(aX + bY, cU + dV) &= ac \cdot Cov(X,U) + ad \cdot Cov(X,V) \\ &\quad + bc \cdot Cov(Y,U) + bd \cdot Cov(Y,V) \end{aligned}$$

If X and Y are independent random variables, then $Cov(X,Y) = 0$.

2.4. Useful Probability Distributions

The definitions in this section are taken from [40] and [97].

2.4.1. Gamma Distribution

The gamma distribution has special importance in probability and statistics.

Definition 2.24. *The gamma function is defined as follow*

$$\Gamma(k) = \int_0^\infty x^{k-1} e^{-x} dx, k \in (0,\infty)$$

The function is well defined, that is, the integral converges for any $k > 0$. On the other hand, the integral diverges to ∞ for $k \leqslant 0$. Two of its key properties are

$$\Gamma(k) = (k-1)\Gamma(k-1)$$

and

$$\Gamma(k)\Gamma(1-k) = \frac{\pi}{sin(\pi k)}$$

Definition 2.25. *A random variable X has the standard gamma distribution with shape parameter* $k \in (0, \infty)$ *if it has the probability density function f given by*

$$f(x) = \frac{1}{\Gamma(k)} x^{k-1} e^{-x} dx, 0 < x < \infty$$

2.4.2. Beta Distribution

Definition 2.26. *The beta function B is defined as follows:*

$$B(a, b) = \int_0^1 u^{a-1}(1-u)^{b-1} du, a > 0, b > 0$$

The beta function is well-defined, that is, $B(a, b) < \infty$ *for any* $a > 0$ *and* $b > 0$.

Definition 2.27. *The beta function can be written in terms of the gamma function as follows:*

$$B(a, b) = \frac{\Gamma(a)\Gamma(b)}{\Gamma(a+b)}; a, b \in (0, \infty)$$

Definition 2.28. *The (standard) beta distribution with left parameter* $a \in (0, \infty)$ *and right parameter* $b \in (0, \infty)$ *is the continuous distribution on* $(0, 1)$ *with probability density function f given by*

$$f(x) = \frac{1}{B(a, b)} x^{a-1}(1-x)^{b-1}, 0 < x < 1$$

2.4.3. Normal approximation to the Beta posterior distribution

The results for the Binomial distributions are both modeling randomness. A Bayesian analysis gives the conveniently simple result s successes in n random trials:

$$p = Beta(s + a, n - s + b)$$

where a $Beta(a, b)$ prior is assumed. The posterior density has the function:

$$f(\theta) \propto \theta^5(1-\theta)^{(n-5)}$$

Taking logs gives:

$$L(\theta) = k + s\log_e[\theta] + (n-s)log_e[1-\theta]$$

and

$$\frac{dL(\theta)}{d\theta} = \frac{s}{\theta} - \frac{n-s}{1-\theta}$$

$$\frac{d^2L(\theta)}{d\theta^2} = -\frac{s}{\theta^2} - \frac{n-s}{(1-\theta)^2}$$

The best estimate q_0 of q will be find:

$$\frac{dL(\theta)}{d\theta}|_{\theta_0} = \frac{s}{\theta_0} - \frac{n-s}{1-\theta_0}$$

which gives:

$$\theta_0 = s/n$$

The standard deviation s for the Normal approximation to this Beta distribution is:

$$\frac{d^2L(\theta)}{d\theta^2}|_{\theta_0} = -\frac{s}{\theta^2} - \frac{n-s}{(1-\theta)^2}$$

which gives:

$$\sigma = \left[\frac{d^2L(\theta)}{d\theta^2}|_{\theta_0}\right]^{1/2} = \left[\frac{\theta_0(1-\theta_0)}{n}\right]^{1/2}$$

and then the approximation is:

$$\theta \approx Normal\left(\theta_0, \left[\frac{\theta_0(1-\theta_0)}{n}\right]^{1/2}\right) = Normal\left(\frac{s}{n}, \left[\frac{s(n-s)}{n^3}\right]^{1/2}\right)$$

2.5. Stratified Sampling

Stratified sampling is based on the idea of iterated expectations [22]. Let Y be a discrete random variable taking values $y_1, y_2, ..., y_L$ with probabilities $p_1, p_2, ..., p_L$. Then,

$$E[X] = E[E[X|Y]] = \sum_{l=1}^{L} E[X|Y = y_l]p_l$$

Suppose that the population can be divided into $L > 1$ groups, known as **strata**. Suppose then that a stratum l contains N_l units from the population ($\sum_{l=1}^{L} N_L = N$), and the value for the units in stratum l are $x_{1l}, x_{2l}, ..., x_{N_l l}$.

Let $W_l = \frac{N_l}{N}$ and $\mu_l = \frac{1}{N_l} \sum_{i=1}^{N_l} x_{il}$, then it follows that the population mean is:

$$\mu = \frac{1}{N} \sum_{l=1}^{L} \sum_{i=1}^{N_l} x_{il} = \frac{1}{N} \sum_{l=1}^{L} N_l \mu_l = \sum_{l=1}^{L} W_l \mu_l$$

Then, instead of taking a simple random sample (SRS) of n units from the total population, we can take a SRS of size n_l from each stratum ($\sum_{l=1}^{L} n_l = n$). Here,

$$\mu_l = E[X|stratum\ \ l]$$
$$W_l = P[Stratum\ ł]$$

so the overall mean satisfies the setup of an iterated expectation.

Let $X_{1l}, X_{2l}, ..., X_{n_l l}$ be a sequence of independent and identically distributed random variables samples from stratum l, the sample mean is defined as:

$$\bar{X_l} = \frac{1}{n_l} \sum_{i=1}^{n_l} X_{il}$$

and the sample variance:

$${S_l}^2 = \frac{1}{n_l - 1} \sum_{i=1}^{n_l} (X_{il} - \bar{X_l})^2$$

Then, an estimate of the population mean μ is:

$$\begin{aligned} \bar{X_S} &= \sum_{l=1}^{L} \frac{N_l}{N} \bar{X_l} \\ &= \sum_{l=1}^{L} W_l \bar{X_l} \\ &= \sum_{l=1}^{L} W_l \frac{1}{n_l} \sum_{i=1}^{n_l} X_{il} \end{aligned}$$

Since, the random variables X_l are independent, then it follows:

$$\begin{aligned} \mathrm{var}(\bar{X_S}) &= \sum_{l=1}^{L} {W_l}^2 Var(\bar{X_l}) \\ &= \sum_{l=1}^{L} {W_l}^2 \frac{1}{n_l} (1 - \frac{n_l - 1}{N_l - 1}) {\sigma_l}^2 \end{aligned}$$

where $\sigma_l^2 = \frac{1}{N_l} \sum_{i=1}^{N_l} (x_{il} - \mu_l)^2$ is the variance of stratum l.

If we assume that $n_l \ll N_l$ for each stratum l so that the finite population factor $FPC = 1 - \frac{n_l - 1}{N_l - 1} \approx 1$ can be ignored, then

$$\mathrm{var}(\bar{X_S}) = \sum_{l=1}^{L} {W_l}^2 \frac{1}{n_l} {\sigma_l}^2 = \frac{1}{N} \sum_{l=1}^{L} {W_l}^2 \frac{{\sigma_l}^2}{a_l}$$

where $a_l = n_l / N$ indicates the fraction of samples drawn from the stratum l.

This variance is controllable through the allocation ratio a_l. For example, the proportional allocation, where $a_l = W_l.N/N = W_l$, yields the variance $\mathrm{var}(\bar{X_{SP}}) = \frac{1}{N} \sum_{l=1}^{L} W_l {\sigma_l}^2$, where $\bar{X}_{SP}$ denotes the sampling mean when proportional sampling is used.

By Lagrange multiplier method, the optimal allocation $a^* := (a_1^*, \ldots, a_L^*)$ is derived in closed form [22]:

$$a_k^* = \frac{W_k.\sigma_k}{\sum_{l=1}^{L} W_l.\sigma_l} \tag{2.22}$$

achieving the minimal variance $\mathrm{var}(X_S^{-}O) = \frac{1}{N}\sum_{l=1}^{L} W_l^2 \frac{\sigma_l^2}{a_l^*} = \frac{1}{N}(\sum_{l=1}^{L} W_l \sigma_l)^2$ [22]. Here, $\bar{X}_{SO}$ denotes the sampling mean when optimal sampling is used.

Moreover, due to the mutual independence of samples across the strata, the empirical mean $\bar{X_S}$ is asymptotically normal [22].

Before, we show which stratified sampling scheme (i.e., random, proportional or optimal) works better, we recall the population variance:

$$\begin{aligned}
\mathrm{var}(X) &= E[\mathrm{var}(X|Stratum)] + \mathrm{var}[E(X|Stratum)] \\
&= \sum_{l=1}^{L} W_l \sigma_l^2 + \sum_{l=1}^{L} W_l(\mu - \mu_l)^2 \\
&= \frac{1}{N}\sum_{l=1}^{L}\sum_{i=1}^{N_l}(x_{il} - \mu)^2 = \sigma^2
\end{aligned}$$

Theorem 2.1.

$$var(\bar{X}_{SP}) \leq var(\bar{X}_S)$$

That is, proportional stratified sampling is never worse than single simple random sample of the same total sample size N

Proof.

$$\begin{aligned}
\mathrm{var}(\bar{X}) - \mathrm{var}(\bar{X}_{SP}) &= \frac{1}{N}(\sum_{i=1}^{L} W_l \sigma_l^2 + \sum_{i=1}^{L} W_l(\mu - \mu_l)^2) - \frac{1}{N}\sum_{l=1}^{L} W_l \sigma_l^2 \\
&= \frac{1}{N}\sum_{i=1}^{L} W_l(\mu - \mu_l)^2 \\
&= \frac{1}{N}\mathrm{var}(E[X|Stratum]) \geq 0
\end{aligned}$$

□

The result of theorem 2.1 means that the more separated the strata means the better is proportional sampling.

Theorem 2.2.

$$var(\bar{X}_{SO}) \leq var(\bar{X}_{SP})$$

That is, optimal stratified sampling is never worse than proportional stratified sample of the same total sample size N

Proof.

$$\begin{aligned}
\mathrm{var}(\bar{X}_{SP}) - \mathrm{var}(\bar{X}_{SO}) &= \frac{1}{N}\sum_{i=1}^{L} W_l {\sigma_l}^2 - \frac{1}{N}(\sum_{l=1}^{L} W_l \sigma_l)^2 \\
&= \frac{1}{N}\sum_{i=1}^{L} W_l(\sigma_l - \bar{\sigma})^2 \\
&= \frac{1}{N}\mathrm{var}(SD[X|Stratum]) \geq 0
\end{aligned}$$

where SD denotes the standard deviation. □

2.6. Active Learning and Uncertainty Sampling

Supervised Learning is an important Machine Learning technique. A Learner learns a predictor or a model by observing value for samples. These samples are provided by the Environment. The input samples and their corresponding values represents the training data.

The choice of a sample is not influenced by the previously observed samples. Learning a predictor is to request the value for a sample drawn at random from a pre-determined distribution.

Furthermore in Active Learning the learner utilizes the information gained from previous observation. Then the learner choose which sample to observe next. The Learner has the flexibility to sample any point form the input domain.

The goal of the Learner is to minimize the number of observed samples required to achieve a certain level of accuracy. Based on the values for samples, the learner decide which samples it should request a value for. Then the learner decide from the environment which samples it should request a value for.

2.7. Bayesian Statistics

Bayesian statistics is a system for describing uncertainty using the mathematical language of probability.

2.7.1. Probability as a Measure of Conditional Uncertainty

The probability $P(E|C)$ is a measure of belief in the occurrence of the event E under conditions C. E is the event whose uncertainty is being measured, and C the conditions under which the measurement takes place. $P(E|D, A, K)$ is to be interpreted as a measure of belief in the occurrence of the event E, given data D, assumptions A and any other available knowledge K.

A survey is conducted to estimate the proportion θ of individuals in a population. Interesting is to use the results from the sample to establish regions of $[0, 1]$ where the unknown value of θ may plausibly be expected to lie. This information is provided by probabilities of the form

$$P(a < \theta < b|r, n, A, K)$$

An experiment is made to count the number r of times that an event E takes place in each of n replications of a well defined situation. E take place r_i times in replication i, and it is desired to forecast the number of times r and E will take place in a future. This is a prediction problem on the value of an observable (discrete) quantity r, given the information provided by data D. Hence, simply the computation of the probabilities $P(r|r_1, ..., r_n, A, K)$, for $r = 0, 1, ...$, is required.

2.7.2. Statistical Inference and Decision Theory

Let A be the class of possible actions. Moreover, for each $a \in A$, let Θ_a be the set of relevant events which may affect the result of choosing a, and let $c(a, \theta) \in C_a$, $\theta \in \Theta_a$, be the consequence of having chosen action a when event θ takes place. $(\Theta_a, C_a), a \in A$ describes the structure of the decision problem.

Different options for the set of acceptable principles:

1. a real-valued bounded utility function $u(c) = u(a, \theta)$ measures the preferences
2. a set of probability distributions $(p(\theta|C, a), \theta \in \Theta_a), a \in A$ measures the uncertainty of relevant events.
3. the expected utility of the available actions measures the desirability

$$u(a|C) = \int_{\Theta_a} u(a, \theta)p(\theta|C, a)d\theta, a \in A$$

It is often convenient to work in terms of the non-negative loss function defined by

$$l(a, \theta) = \sup_{a \in A} u(a, \theta) - u(a, \theta),$$

which directly measures, as a function of θ. The relative undesirability of available actions $a \in A$ is then measured by their expected loss

$$l(a|C) = \int_{\Theta_a} l(a, \theta)p(\theta|C, a)d\theta, a \in A$$

2.8. Symbolic Execution

The white-box reliability assessment approach we present in this thesis bases mainly on the ability to symbolically execute the code under consideration. Algorithm 1 shows an abstract procedure of our symbolic execution. For a given program starting with statement s and an initial update $\mathcal{U}_0$, the call of *symExe*($\mathcal{U}_0$, *s*, *true*, $\emptyset$) will return the path conditions of all feasible paths of the program. Until a branching condition is found the procedure accumulates the state changes in form of update expressions (lines 5-7). In the case of a branching statement a new path condition is constructed for each branch outcome based of the current path condition Φ and the branch conditions ($cond(s)$ and $\neg cond(s)$). Only if a constructed path condition is satisfiable, the corresponding branch code is further proceeded (lines 8-11).

Here, we give an abstract formalism for what is meant with symbolic execution. For simplicity, we abstract from real programming languages and categorize program statements s to branching statements, if $branch(s) = true$ and non branching statements, otherwise. The next scheduled statement after a statement s is denoted by $next(s)$ and is possibly empty. For a branching statement s we further define its branching condition as $cond(s)$ and the first statement of its body as $first(s)$. The state updates cause during the symbolic execution are captured using update expressions $\mathcal{U}$. The state update causes by a single statement s is denoted by $update(s)$. Updates concatenations are denoted by "$\circ$". The evaluation of a formula Φ with respect to an update $\mathcal{U}$ is denoted by $\{\mathcal{U}\}\Phi$.

Algorithm 1: An abstract symbolic execution procedure – symExe

```
   Data: 𝒰 : Update, s : Statement, Φ : Formula, PCs : Set<Formula>
   Result: PCs : Set<Formula>
1  begin
2      if s = ∅ then
3          PCs ← PCs ∪ Φ
4      else
5          while ¬branch(s) do
6              𝒰 ← 𝒰 ∘ update(s)
7              s ← next(s)
8          if SAT(Φ ∧ {𝒰}cond(s)) then
9              symExe(𝒰, first(s), Φ ∧ {𝒰}cond(s), PCs)
10         if SAT(Φ ∧ {𝒰}¬cond(s)) then
11             symExe(𝒰, next(s), Φ ∧ {𝒰}¬cond(s), PCs)
12         return PCs
```

For example, the constraint solver can decide that the following constraint is satisfiable: $(x \geq 10) \wedge ((x < 5) \vee (x > 90))$. The constraint solver can found a solution, e.g., $x = 95$. The found solution can serve as an input value in a test case. When the program path is executable, i.e., the corresponding path condition is satisfiable, one can ask how many possible input values satisfy the path condition. Generally, the more inputs satisfy the path condition, the more probable the path can be executed. We discuss this intuition in the next section. Note that the symbolic execution description in Algo. 1, does not address performance issues. Especially the incremental call of the solver on incrementally extended conjunctions (lines 8 and 10) can make use of the incremental solving ability supported by most solvers, e.g., Z3 [31].

2.9. KeY Verification Approach

KeY [7] is an interactive software verification system which can verify sequential Java programs specified with the Java Modeling Language. It uses a sequent calculus for JavaDL [7], a dynamic logic for Java. JavaDL extends first-order logic with modal operators such as $\langle p \rangle$ for every program p. The formula $\langle p \rangle \varphi$ means that the formula φ is true in the state after executing p, hence φ is the postcondition of p. During the verification process, KeY creates a proof tree, with sequents as nodes. A sequent typical has the form $\Gamma \Rightarrow \langle p \rangle \varphi$, where Γ is a comma-separated conjunction of conditions which constitute a path condition. As part of the verification process, KeY symbolically executes the program, thus taking all possible execution paths into consideration. Besides formal verification, KeY also provides a basis for complementary approaches like testing, and can generate test cases with high coverage from a proof.

3. Adaptive Constrained Statistical Testing

In this chapter we consider the case where the only information we have about the software under study is the operational profile $OP = \{(\mathcal{D}_i, p_i) | i = \{1, 2, \ldots, L\}, \sum_{i=1}^{L} p_i = 1\}$. In this case, we treat the software as a black-box. Our goal in this chapter is to create a test selection approach which should outperform existing current practices in the sense that it reduces the number of required test cases to be executed in order to reach a target statistical confidence on the reliability estimate. The approach we present here makes use of novel mathematical sampling models and information theoretic principles to efficiently select the test cases to be executed while the only information provided to the approach is the operational profile of the software under study.

Before we discuss our approach, it is necessary to introduce some related terms. The input domain of a software represents all relevant inputs to the execution of the software. The operational profile sub-domains represents subsets of the input domain. A sub-domain is homogeneous if either all of its elements cause the software to succeed or all cause it to fail. Consequently, any input from a homogeneous sub-domain is a good representation of the entire sub-domain. A sub-domain is heterogeneous if some (but not all) of its elements cause the software to fail.

3.1. Problem Definition

Statistical testing based on sampling models is theoretical sound but requires a huge number of test cases to reach a target statistical confidence on the unknown reliability estimate, if testing reveals failures. Existing approaches for sampling based statistical testing are formulating testing as proportional stratified sampling process (see Section 2.1.3), and are not making use of the information provided by previous testing effort.

The main idea behind standard statistical testing approaches is to ensure that when the testing process is terminated because of (for example) imperative software project constraints, then the most used operations will have received the most testing effort. Musa also claims that "the reliability level will be the maximum that is practically achievable for the given test time" [69]. However, the reliability estimate of such approaches may be inaccurate, when testing reveals failures. Indeed, the reliability estimate across the operational profile sub-domains may have different statistical properties (i.e., mean and variance). This means that the operational profile sub-domains may be heterogeneous in regard to the failure rate. Using conventional proportional random sampling to select test cases from heterogeneous sub-domains does not guarantee that a statistically sufficient number of test cases will be selected from every sub-domain (see theorem 2.2). Hence, the statistical quality of the samples may be compromised for some sub-domains. This may lead to inaccurate statistical estimate. The accuracy of the reliability estimate, since it is a random variable, is measured by its variance. In order to increase the accuracy of the reliability estimate, further test cases are needed to be executed to reduce the variance.

It would be ideal if we could separate successful program execution from the failing ones. However, this is not likely, because failures are often caused by faults in a large program. A software fault is a hidden programming error in one or more program statements. A program consists of a set of statements. A program execution is a program path executed with an input value from the program's input domain. A program path is a sequence of statements. Each program path has an input and an executed output which usually depends on the input. Consequently, a program execution is considered as a failure if the corresponding executed program path deviates from the expected output. Two similar software executions may differ only whether a fault is reached or not. Two program execution are similar if they execute the same program path with different input value, if the same input value is used then the two executions are equal. Two similar program executions may differ only in regard to executing a particular fault, with the result that one execution fails while the other does not. Conversely, two dissimilar program execution may both fail because they execute the same faulty program statement. Consequently. we may not group if the failing program executions together even if they have the same causing fault. Hence, it is realistic to assume that the reliability estimate across the test sub-domains have different statistical properties (i.e., mean and variance).

For a given test budget, optimal stratified sampling as shown in theorem 2.2, can estimate the reliability with less variance than proportional stratified sampling, especially when the variability between the sub-domains is high. In this chapter, we formulate statistical testing as an optimal stratified sampling process. In order, to learn from previous testing effort, we formulate testing as an active learning problem.

3.2. Idea of the Approach

Software reliability assessment based on testing formulates software testing as a statistical inference task as explained in Section 2.1.3. The goal of the inference task is to estimate the reliability of the software by using a statistical estimator specific to the inference task. Main focus when doing statistical inference is to reduce the variance of the estimate as possible.

The variance of an estimator describes the closeness of the future estimate to the previous estimate when rerunning the estimation with the same setting. An estimator with low variance increases the confidence on the predicted estimate. In fact, a low variance usually implies tighter confidence interval for the estimate. Consequently, we can improve the accuracy of the reliability estimation by minimizing the variance of the estimator.

The result of an estimation is a sum of the true value to be estimated and a random error. The lower the variance is, the more likely the error will be close to zero. Therefore, the variance of the estimator should be lowered as possible to restrict the error to an enough tight interval in order to provide an accurate enough estimate. It is also important to note that the more tests are executed the more will the variance of the estimator decrease. Consequently, an estimator with low variance can find an accurate estimation with fewer test cases.

Stratified sampling is a statistical technique to reduce the variance of an estimator. Optimal stratified sampling is shown to reduce the variance of the estimator more than proportional sampling, especially when the variability between the strata (sub-domains in our case) is high. Consequently, by choosing the proportional stratified sampling to sample the operational profile, we may sacrifice a possible efficiency we could obtain when using optimal stratified sampling.

We developed a test selection approach which is based on active learning toward optimal stratified sampling. For a required statistical confidence on the reliability estimate, our approach computes the number of test cases to execute from each sub-domain. If the selected test cases revealed failures, the responsible faults are repaired, and the approach recomputes the number of test cases to execute. The number of test cases to execute from each sub-domain of the operational profile is computed based on the uncertainty reduction principle of active learning.

We proved in theorem 3.2, that our approach asymptotically converges to optimal sampling. Consequently, for a given test time, our approach delivers a reliability estimate with lower variance than state-of-the-art existing approaches, which are based on proportional sampling. This also means, for a required statistical confidence on the reliability estimate, our approach can estimate the true unknown reliability with less test cases than standard approaches.

3.3. Research Goals and Challenges

Software reliability testing is a continuous process: the software is frozen and tested based on the given operational profile to estimate its current reliability. Usually, the reliability tester wants to estimate the reliability of the software with a required confidence and up to a maximal allowed margin of estimation error. The number of required test cases to reach the target confidence and margin of error are not known in advance. Statistical hypothesis testing can be used to estimate the number of test cases that should be executed failure-free to reach the target reliability with the required confidence. However, when testing revealed failures, than the responsible faults should be repaired and testing should be re-executed with same number of test cases initially computed using hypothesis testing. This process should be iterated until the required confidence on the estimated reliability is reached.

The continuous nature of testing possibly heterogeneous software executions for reliability estimation introduces the following additional challenges. First, the number of of required test cases executions from each sub-domain as well as the statistical properties (i.e., mean and variance of the failure rate) of the software when executed with inputs from each sub-domain are not known in advance. Consequently, it is not possible to optimally allocate a stratified sample of test cases to the operational profile sub-domains prior sampling. Second, the statistical properties of the sub-domains may change over testing time. Hence, the allocation should be able to adapt to such changes.

The approach we present here addresses the problem of allocating a stratified sample of test cases over heterogeneous operational profile sub-domains to deliver an unbiased low variance reliability estimator. There are four challenges in this problem. The first challenge is to allocate the test cases optimally among the sub-domains while not knowing the total number of test cases in advance. The optimality criteria is the estimator quality (i.e., mean and variance). We solve this issue by adopting the Neyman method [97] for optimal allocation in stratified sampling. This method method assumes, however, that the sample size is fix. We present an adaptive version of this method to account for the unknown sample size. The second issue is to account for the probability of occurrence of each sub-domain while allocating the test cases optimally over the sub-domains. The intuition behind software statistical testing is that the higher the probability of occurrence of a sub-domain, the larger the number of test cases will be executed from that sub-domain. We solve this issue by constraining the adaptive optimal allocation with a utility cost function. The cost for selecting a test case from a sub-domain is defined as the inverse probability of the probability of occurrence of the sub-domain. The third issue is to quantify the similarity of the selected test cases over the sub-domains to the operational profile. Test cases executions simulate the expected software behavior according to the operational profile. We define a similarity confidence metric and we provide an approach to adjust the test cases allocation toward 100% similarity confidence. The fourth issue is to determine when to stop testing. We present a test stopping criteria based on the software tester required (i) confidence on the reliability estimate, and (ii) the maximal margin of estimation error. We call the algorithm solving this issues adaptive constrained statistical testing.

We have published part of the following results in [72].

3.4. Assumptions

In order to formulate the concerned research goal, some assumptions on the software are presented.

1. The software is frozen when estimating the reliability, since reliability estimation aims at testing the current status of the software. The software will not be modified during the estimation process. The software can be modified after the estimation process.
2. The output of each test is independent of the testing history. In some cases, it is possible that a test case is judged to be failure free although it actually leads to some faults which cannot be observed due to limited test oracles. We consider such test cases to be failure free. However, such unobserved faulty program states can cause the failure of some following test cases. Consequently, the latter test cases can be mistakenly considered as faulty test cases. This leads to an error in the reliability estimation. However, this is not a reliability estimation approach concern rather is a test oracle problem.
3. Each test case either fails or succeeds. A test oracle is used to verify the behavior of the software under test.
4. We assume that a proper test oracle is available, since this work focuses on the effectiveness and efficiency of reliability estimation.
5. We assume that failures are uniformly distributed over the sub-domains. This assumption is inherited from the principle of stratified sampling and random sampling as presented in Section 2.5.
6. In each operational use represented by a sub-domain $\mathcal{D}_i$, all possible software operations and possible inputs are equally likely to arise.
7. We assume that an operational profile is provided for the tested software.

3.5. The Statistical Model for Reliability Estimation

The $OP = \{(D_i, p_i) | i \in \{1, ..., L\}, \sum_{i=1}^{L} p_i = 1\}$ defines the expected input domain of the program's input variables. Each partition (D_l, p_l) is a subset of the OP, and $p_l \geq 0$ is the probability that a program input belongs to sub-domain D_l. The OP is a natural definition of the strata for stratified random sampling. Each stratum l corresponds to the sub-domain $\mathcal{D}_l$ and has a weight $W_l = p_l$.

Based on assumption 3, each test case execution is a Bernoulli trial. Let $X_{i,l}$ be the outcome of test case t_i from sub-domain $\mathcal{D}_l$, then:

$$X_{i,l} = \begin{cases} 1, & \text{if test case } t_i \text{ fails} \\ 0, & \text{if test case } t_i \text{ not fails} \end{cases}.$$

Let $\mu_i = \mathbb{P}(\text{test cases from sub-domain } \mathcal{D}_i \text{ fail})$ be the probability of failure on demand when the software system is executed with inputs from $\mathcal{D}_i$, where $i = \{1, 2, \ldots, L\}$ and $\mu_i \in [0, 1]$.

Based on assumption 2, $\{X_{i,l}\}$ are independent random variables, and since $\sum_{i=1}^{L} p_i = 1$, then it can inferred that $P(X_{i,l} = 1) = \mu_i$ (i.e., the probability that test case i from sub-domain $\mathcal{D}_l$ fails). Each test case will lead the software under test to failure or success. And in each sub-domain the probability of failure of each test case is equal for all test cases in the sub-domain. Hence the distribution of X_{il} is Binomial with μ_i. Thus, the number of failures in n demands executed with inputs from sub-domain $\mathcal{D}_l$, has a Binomial distribution:

$$\mathbb{P}(X_l = k) = \binom{n}{k} \mu_l^k (1 - \mu_l)^{n-k} \tag{3.1}$$

and in particular

$$\mathbb{P}(X_l = 0) = (1 - \mu_l)^n \tag{3.2}$$

Consequently, the sample mean of the failure on demand when using inputs from sub-domain $\mathcal{D}_l$,

$$\bar{X}_l = \frac{1}{n_l}\sum_{i=1}^{n_l} X_{il} \tag{3.3}$$

is an unbiased point estimator of μ_i. Thus, μ_i is Binomial distributed.

The reliability of the tested software can be defined as the weighted sum of the reliability of the sampled OP sub-domains $\mathcal{D}_{i,\ \{i\in\{1,\ldots,L\}\}}$: $R = \sum_{i=1}^{L} p_i(1-\mu_i)$. An unbiased estimator of the reliability is then defined as:

$$\widehat{R} = 1 - \sum_{i=1}^{L} p_i\bar{X}_i = 1 - \sum_{l=1}^{L} \frac{1}{n_l}.p_l \sum_{i=1}^{n_l} X_{il} \tag{3.4}$$

Since the distribution of X_{il} is a binomial distribution with μ_i it follows:

$$E[\widehat{R}] = 1 - \sum_{i=1}^{L} p_i\hat{\mu}_i \tag{3.5a}$$

$$\text{var}[\widehat{R}] = \sum_{i=1}^{L} {p_i}^2 \frac{\hat{\mu}_i.(1-\hat{\mu}_i)}{n_i} = \sum_{i=1}^{L} {p_i}^2 \frac{{\sigma_i}^2}{n_i} \tag{3.5b}$$

where $\hat{\mu}_i$ an estimation of the true failure rate μ_i and ${\sigma_i}^2$ its variance. The goal of the next sections is to show how $\hat{\mu}_i$ and ${\sigma_i}^2$ are iteratively computed to actively compute the required number of test cases to select from each sub-domain $\mathcal{D}_i$ at each iteration.

3.6. Optimal Test Cases Selection

The Problem of selecting the test cases optimally from the OP sub-domains is an adaptive optimization problem formulated as follows. Given the OP, we want to select a total number n of test cases, where (i) n_i test cases are selected from each sub-domains $\mathcal{D}_{i\,i\in\{1,\ldots,L\}}$ and (ii) $\sum_{i=1}^{L} n_i = n$, with the goal to minimize var$[\hat{R}]$. For mathematical tractability, we assume in this section that the total number of required test case n as well as the sub-domains failure rates σ_i and consequently their variances are known. In the next sections, we will show how n and σ_i are computed actively in an adaptive manner. According to Section 2.5:

$$n_i = n \frac{p_i \sigma_i}{\sum_{k=1}^{L} p_k \sigma_k} \tag{3.6}$$

Note that the larger the variance ${\sigma_i}^2$ of the failure rate of the software when executed with inputs from the sub-domain $\mathcal{D}_i$, the more test cases should be selected from that sub-domain. This makes sense, since the sub-domain with higher estimated/observed failure rate variability should require more testing to attain the same degree of precision as those with lower variability. If the variances of all sub-domains are all equal, the optimal allocation is proportional allocation.

Consequently, by sampling the OP proportionally to their probabilities of occurrence, we assume implicitly that the failure rate (i.e, their variances) are all equal. This a hart-to-justify assumption, since we do not know the failure rates of the software in advance, neither can we realistically find a partition of the software input domain that guarantees equal or quasi-equal failure rate across the partitions. In contrary, we may know from previous software testing experience that some operations in the software are expected to have a bigger failure rate than other operations. In addition, when using Commercial Off-the-Shelf (COTS) software for example, we usually do not know the level of quality of the integrated COTS software and consequently we usually assume that the operations implementing the integration logic with the COTS software are likely to have a big failure rate. Intuitively, a software tester would focus his test cases on the parts of the software where the most failures are observed. This intuition is incarnated in the principle of optimal stratified sampling.

3.7. Constrained Optimal Selection

The intuition behind statistical testing is that the highest the probability of occurrence of a sub-domain, the larger the number of test cases executed from that sub-domain.

To account for this, the optimal allocation introduced in the previous section is formulated as a constrained optimization to a utility cost function c^* defined as follows. Let $c_i = 1 - p_i$ the cost of selecting a test case from a sub-domain $\mathcal{D}_i$ that has a probability of occurrence p_i, and the overall cost of testing defined as:

$$c^* = \sum_{i=1}^{L} c_i n_i \tag{3.7}$$

The goal is to minimize the variance of the reliability estimate defined in equation (3.5b) as:

$$\text{var}[\widehat{R}] = \sum_{i=1}^{L} {p_i}^2 \frac{\mu_i.(1-\mu_i)}{n_i} = \sum_{i=1}^{L} {p_i}^2 \frac{{\sigma_i}^2}{n_i} \tag{3.8}$$

by selecting appropriate number of test cases n_i with respect to the cost function defined in equation (3.7).

We derive the appropriate number of test cases n_i using a Lagrange multiplier technique.

Based on equations (3.5b, 3.7) we form the following Lagrangian:

$$\mathcal{L} = \sum_{i=1}^{L} {p_i}^2 \frac{{\sigma_i}^2}{n_i} - \lambda(\sum_{i=1}^{L} c_i n_i - c^*) \tag{3.9}$$

By taking the first derivate to n_i and λ and setting them to 0 we obtain:

$$\frac{-{p_i}^2{\sigma_i}^2}{{n_i}^2} + \lambda c_i = 0, \quad i = 1\ldots, L \tag{3.10a}$$

$$c^* = \sum_{i=1}^{L} c_i n_i \tag{3.10b}$$

Rearranging equation (3.10a) gives:

$$n_i = \frac{1}{\sqrt{\lambda}} \frac{p_i \sigma_i}{\sqrt{c_i}} \qquad i = 1 \ldots, L \tag{3.11}$$

Now we use the cost function in equation (3.7) to solve for $\frac{1}{\sqrt{\lambda}}$:

$$c^* = \sum_{i=1}^{L} c_i n_i = \frac{1}{\sqrt{\lambda}} \sum_{i=1}^{L} c_i \frac{p_i \sigma_i}{\sqrt{c_i}} \tag{3.12a}$$

$$= \frac{1}{\sqrt{\lambda}} \sum_{i=1}^{L} \sqrt{c_i} p_i \sigma_i \tag{3.12b}$$

Consequently, it follows:

$$\frac{1}{\sqrt{\lambda}} = \frac{c^*}{\sum_{i=1}^{L} \sqrt{c_i} p_i \sigma_i} \tag{3.13}$$

Substituting equation (3.13) in equation (3.11) leads to:

$$n_i = c^* . \frac{p_i \sigma_i / \sqrt{c_i}}{\sum_{k=1}^{L} p_k \sigma_k / \sqrt{c_k}} \tag{3.14}$$

Note, that the higher the cost c_i of selecting a test case from sub-domain $\mathcal{D}_i$, the smaller the sub-domain sample size n_i.

Since the cost function c_i is defined as $c_i = 1 - p_i$ then equation 3.14 means: the smaller the probability of occurrence of a sub-domain $\mathcal{D}_i$, the less test cases n_i will be selected from $\mathcal{D}_i$.

3.8. Similarity Confidence

When testing a software according to an operational profile, the goal is to simulate the expected software execution as described by the operational profile. Consequently, it is interesting to quantify the similarity of the total set of selected test cases to the expected operational profile. It is also interesting to control the testing process toward a 100% similarity to the operational profile.

Let $\mathcal{T}_{\mathcal{D}_i}$ be the set of test cases selected from the sub-domain $\mathcal{D}_{i\,\{i\in 1,\ldots,L\}}$. Let $|\mathcal{T}_{\mathcal{D}_i}| = n_i$, i.e., the set $\mathcal{T}_{\mathcal{D}_i}$ contains n_i different test cases selected from the sub-domain $\mathcal{D}_{i\,\{i\in 1,\ldots,L\}}$. Let $\mathcal{T}_{OP} = \{\mathcal{T}_{(\mathcal{D}_i,p_i)} | (\mathcal{D}_i,p_i) \in OP = \{(\mathcal{D}_i,p_i) | i \in \{1,\ldots,L\}, \sum_{i=1}^{L} p_i = 1\}\}$ the set of selected test cases from the operational profile. The similarity of $\mathcal{T}_{(\mathcal{D}_i,p_i)}$ to the OP when a total number $n = |\bigcup_{\mathcal{D}_i \in OP} \mathcal{T}_{\mathcal{D}_i}| = |\mathcal{T}_{OP}|$ of test cases is selected from the operational profile sub-domains, is defined as follows:

$$\mathcal{SC}(\mathcal{T}_{\mathcal{D}_i}) = \begin{cases} \frac{n_i}{\lceil p_i.n \rceil}, & \text{if } n_i \leq \lceil p_i.n \rceil \\ -\frac{n_i}{\lceil p_i.n \rceil}, & \text{if } n_i > \lceil p_i.n \rceil \end{cases} \tag{3.15}$$

The similarity confidence of the total selected test cases is consequently defined as follows:

$$\mathcal{SC}(\bigcup_{\mathcal{D}_i \in OP} \mathcal{T}_{\mathcal{D}_i}) = \frac{\sum_{i=1}^{L} \mathcal{SC}(\mathcal{T}_{\mathcal{D}_i})}{L} \tag{3.16}$$

Let $\mathcal{SC}_{min} = min\{\mathcal{SC}(\mathcal{T}_{\mathcal{D}_i}) | i \in \{1,\ldots,L\}\} = \mathcal{SC}(\mathcal{T}_{\mathcal{D}_k})_{k\in\{1,\ldots,L\}}$, the minimum computed similarity to the operational profile.

Algorithm 2: Adjust to Proportional Sampling

```
if SC(T_OP) ≠ 1 ∧ SC_min = SC(T_(D_k,p_k)) < 0 then
  n = ⌈n_k/p_k⌉ T_(D_k,p_k) is over-proportional sampled
  for T_(D_i,p_i) ∈ T ∧ T_(D_i,p_i) ≠ T_(D_k,p_k) do
    n_i = ⌈n.p_i⌉
    //select extra (⌈n.p_i⌉ − n_i) test cases
  end for
else
  for T_(D_i,p_i) ∈ T do
    n_i = ⌈n.p_i⌉
  end for
end if
```

Algorithm 2, adjusts the allocation of the test cases from each sub-domain $\mathcal{D}_{i\{i\in 1,...,L\}}$ to reach a similarity confidence of 100%. The steps of the algorithm are as follows. If the selected tested cases $\mathcal{T}_{OP}$ is not similar to the OP and if $\mathcal{SC}_{min} = SC(D_k)$ is negative (line 1), then it means that the sub-domain $\mathcal{D}_k$ is over proportionally sampled. In this case, the total number of test case n is updated proportionally to n_k (line 3), and for each sub-domain except the sub-domain $\mathcal{D}_k$, extra $(\lceil n.p_i \rceil - n_i)$ test case are selected (lines 4-6).

Otherwise, the sub-domains are under proportionally sampled, and for each sub-domain $\mathcal{D}_i$, extra $(\lceil n.p_i \rceil - n_i)$ test case are selected (lines 8-9).

3.9. Bayesian Inference and Stopping Criteria

We define a test stopping criteria based on the tester required (i) maximal error of the reliability estimate d, and (ii) confidence level $(1 - \alpha)$. The goal of reliability testing is then to estimate the reliability $\hat{R}$ to within d with $100(1 - \alpha)\%$ confidence.

For any test case t_i selected from sub-domain $\mathcal{D}_l$, we can according to assumption 3, deterministically decide its outcome X_{il} (i.e., whether t_i fails or not). Let $u_l = \mathbb{P}(\text{test cases from } \mathcal{D}_l \text{ fail})$, be the probability of failure on demand as introduced in Section 3.5. The outcome X_{il} is a Bernoulli random variable according to assumption 2. Thus, the conditional probability density function associated with X_{il} is:

$$f(X_{il}|\mu_l) = \mu_l^{X_{il}}(1 - \mu_l)^{1-X_{il}} \tag{3.17}$$

Within the Bayesian framework, we assume that μ_l is given by a random variable M_l over $(0, 1)$, whose density $f(.)$ is called the *prior* density. The prior is a representation of a knowledge based on previous experiences or beliefs about the parameter of interest, here μ_l.

Based on equation 3.3, μ_l is Binomial distributed. The conjugate prior to the Binomial distribution is the Beta distribution. Consequently, we use the Beta distribution for the prior density of μ_l. The advantage in using a prior distribution from the conjugate family is that both prior and posterior distributions are members of the same parametric distribution family. This allows us to have a kind of homogeneity in the way the belief about μ_l changes as extra information are received. Thus, the conjugate distribution is the Beta(β_1, β_2) distribution:

$$\mu_l \sim Beta(\beta_1, \beta_2) \tag{3.18a}$$

$$f(\mu_l) = \frac{\mu_l^{\beta_1 - 1}(1 - \mu_l)^{\beta_2 - 1}}{B(\beta_1, \beta_2)} \tag{3.18b}$$

$$\propto \mu_l^{\beta_1 - 1}(1 - \mu_l)^{\beta_2 - 1} \tag{3.18c}$$

where the approximation in equation (3.18c) is the result of ignoring the constant of proportionality represented by the Beta function $B(\beta_1, \beta_2)$. The beta function is parameterized with the two parameters $\beta_1 > 0$, $\beta_2 > 0$ representing the belief about μ_l prior seeing any test results:

$$B(\beta_1, \beta_2) = \int_0^1 u^{\beta_1 - 1}(1 - u)^{\beta_2 - 1} du \tag{3.19}$$

By exploiting the relationship between the beta function and the gamma function (see Section 2.4.2), namely that:

$$B(\beta_1, \beta_2) = \frac{\Gamma(\beta_1)\Gamma(\beta_2)}{\Gamma(\beta_1 + \beta_2)} \tag{3.20}$$

it follows:

$$f(\mu_l) = \frac{\Gamma(\beta_1 + \beta_2)}{\Gamma(\beta_1)\Gamma(\beta_2)} \mu_l^{\beta_1 - 1}(1 - \mu_l)^{\beta_2 - 1} \tag{3.21}$$

The prior distribution summarizes all the information —including its lack— gathered through testing about the failure probability μ_l. The prior is parameterized based on previous experience and information about the software systems and its development process. One way to encode such knowledge is to parameterize β_1 and β_2 as follows:

$$\beta_1 = \hat{\mu}_l \mathcal{T} \tag{3.22a}$$

$$\beta_2 = (1 - \hat{\mu}_l)\mathcal{T} \tag{3.22b}$$

where $\hat{\mu}_l$ is an initial knowledge-based or experience-based estimate of the true and unknown failure probability μ_l, and $\mathcal{T} \geq 1$ represents a trust factor. The trust factor is specified based on knowledge and previous observations about the software system. We propose as in [40], to set the trust factor $\mathcal{T}$ to the number of test cases executed to get the initial estimate of $\hat{\mu}_l$.

In some cases, however, such information may not be available. In such a case, the *non-informative* or *ignorance* uniform prior with $\beta_1 = \beta_2 = 1$ can be used.

Suppose now that n test cases $t_i, \ldots, t_n$ from sub-domain $\mathcal{D}_l$ are executed. The test cases has the outcome $X_{1,l}, \ldots, X_{n,l}$. Suppose that k failures are observed, meaning $\sum_{i=1}^{n} X_{i,l} = k$. The posterior distribution over μ_l is then given by:

$$
\begin{aligned}
f(\mu_l | \sum_{i=1}^{n} X_{i,l} = k, \beta_1, \beta_2) &= \frac{f(\sum_{i=1}^{n} X_{i,l} = k | \mu_l) f(\mu_l)}{\int_0^1 f(\sum_{i=1}^{n} X_{i,l} = k | \omega) f(\omega) d\omega} && (3.23a) \\
&\propto f(\sum_{i=1}^{n} X_{i,l} = k | \mu_l) f(\mu_l) && (3.23b) \\
&= \binom{n}{k} \mu_l^k (1 - \mu_l)^{n-k} && (3.23c) \\
&\times \frac{\Gamma(\beta_1 + \beta_2)}{\Gamma(\beta_1)\Gamma(\beta_2)} \mu_l^{\beta_1 - 1} (1 - \mu_l)^{\beta_2 - 1} && (3.23d) \\
&\propto \mu_l^k (1 - \mu_l)^{n-k} \times \mu_l^{\beta_1 - 1} (1 - \mu_l)^{\beta_2 - 1} && (3.23e) \\
&= \mu_l^{k + \beta_1 - 1} (1 - \mu_l)^{n - k + \beta_2 - 1} && (3.23f)
\end{aligned}
$$

Note that the approximations in equation (3.23b) and equation (3.23e) are the result when ignoring the constants of proportionality.

Recall equation (3.18c), it follows from equation (3.23) then:

$$
\mu_l | \sum_{i=1}^{n} X_{i,l} = k \sim Beta(\beta_1 + k, \beta_2 + n - k) \tag{3.24}
$$

Equation (3.24) describes the *conjugacy* property. The conjugacy property together with the Bayes theorem are used to update the prior information on the probability μ_l after each iteration of our approach. This leads to the construction of the posterior distribution of μ_l which will be used for statistical estimation of the reliability $\hat{R}$ as explained below.

Recall the stopping criteria: for a given test budget, we want to stop reliability testing as soon as the reliability is estimated with a confidence level of $1 - \alpha$, with a margin of error d. This means, we want to compute $E[\hat{R}]$ such that:

$$\mathbb{P}(E[\hat{R}] - d \leq R \leq E[\hat{R}] + d) \geq 1 - \alpha \tag{3.25}$$

where $E[\widehat{R}] = 1 - \sum_{i=1}^{L} p_i \hat{\mu}_i$.

In Section 3.9.1, we show how we estimate iteratively the failure rate $\hat{\mu_i}$ as well its variance σ_i for each sub-domain $\mathcal{D}_{i, i \in \{1,\ldots,L\}}$. Then, in Section 3.9.2, we show how we use the failure rate to compute the required number of test cases to select from each sub-domain $\mathcal{D}_{i, i \in \{1,\ldots,L\}}$ based on the user target confidence level $1 - \alpha$ and margin of error d.

3.9.1. Iterative Estimation of the Failure Rate pro Sub-Domain

According to Bayes theorem, each test case executed from a sub-domain $\mathcal{D}_l$ is a sample from a density $f(.|\mu_l)$. Recall that μ_l is an unknown probability given by the random variable M_l whose density is $f(.)$ as given in equation 3.18. Consequently, the posterior density of M_l after executing the test cases $t_1, \ldots, t_n$, whose outcome is $X_{1l}, \ldots, X_{nl}$ is:

$$f(\mu_l | X_{1l}, \ldots, X_{nl}) = \frac{f(X_{1l}, \ldots, X_{nl} | \mu_l) f(\mu_l)}{\int_0^1 f(X_{1l}, \ldots, X_{nl} | \omega) f(\omega) d\omega} \tag{3.26}$$

Based on assumption 2 of our approach (the independence of the test cases outputs), it follows:

$$f(\mu_l | X_{1l}, \ldots, X_{nl}) = \frac{\prod_{i=1}^{n} f(X_{il} | \mu_l) f(\mu_l)}{\int_0^1 f(X_{1l}, \ldots, X_{nl} | \omega) f(\omega) d\omega} \tag{3.27}$$

where $f(X_{il}|\mu_l)$, introduced in equation 3.17, is the conditional density function associated with the $i-th$ test case executed from sub-domain $\mathcal{D}_l$.

Since the posterior density of M_l is a distribution (see equations 3.26 and 3.27), we can estimate μ_l by the posterior mean based on the result we got from equation (3.24), which indicates that the posterior distribution of μ_l is $Beta(\beta_1 + k, \beta_2 + n - k)$. By using the property of the Gamma function $\Gamma(x + 1) = x\Gamma(x)$ (See Section 2.4.1), the posterior mean is:

$$\hat{\mu_l} = E[\mu_l | \sum_{i=1}^{n} X_{i,l} = k, \beta_1, \beta_2] \tag{3.28a}$$

$$= \int_0^1 \mu_l f(\mu_l | \sum_{i=1}^{n} X_{i,l} = k, \beta_1, \beta_2) d\mu_l \tag{3.28b}$$

$$= \int_0^1 \mu_l \frac{\Gamma(\beta_1 + \beta_2 + n)}{\Gamma(\beta_1 + k)\Gamma(\beta_2 + n - k)} \mu_l^{\beta_1+k-1} (1 - \mu_l)^{\beta_2+n-k-1} d\mu_l \tag{3.28c}$$

$$= \frac{\Gamma(\beta_1 + \beta_2 + n)}{\Gamma(\beta_1 + k)\Gamma(\beta_2 + n - k)} \int_0^1 \mu_l^{\beta_1+k} (1 - \mu_l)^{\beta_2+n-k-1} d\mu_l \tag{3.28d}$$

$$= \frac{\Gamma(\beta_1 + \beta_2 + n)}{\Gamma(\beta_1 + k)\Gamma(\beta_2 + n - k)} \times \frac{\Gamma(\beta_1 + k + 1)\Gamma(\beta_2 + n - k)}{\Gamma(\beta_1 + \beta_2 + n + 1)} \tag{3.28e}$$

$$= \frac{\Gamma(\beta_1 + k + 1)}{\Gamma(\beta_1 + k)} \times \frac{\Gamma(\beta_1 + \beta_2 + n)}{\Gamma(\beta_1 + \beta_2 + n + 1)} \tag{3.28f}$$

$$= \frac{\beta_1 + k}{\beta_1 + \beta_2 + n} \tag{3.28g}$$

The variance of μ_l is then computed based on the above equation (3.28g) and by means of few algebraic steps as follows:

$$var[\mu_l] = E[{\mu_l}^2] - (E[\mu_l])^2 \tag{3.29a}$$

$$= \frac{(\beta_1 + k)(\beta_2 + n_l - k)}{(\beta_1 + \beta_2 + n_l)^2(\beta_1 + \beta_2 + n_l + 1)} \tag{3.29b}$$

3.9.2. Iterative Computation of the Number of Test Cases to Select

As shown in Section 2.4.3, we can approximate the Beta distribution $Beta(\beta_1, \beta_2)$ to a normal distribution.

Now, recall that after executing n_l test cases from a sub-domain $\mathcal{D}_l$, where k test cases failed, the distribution of the failure rate μ_l is given by equation (3.24): $\mu_l | \sum_{i=1}^{n_l} X_{i,l} = k \sim Beta(\beta_1 + k, \beta_2 + n_l - k)$.

Consequently, we can approximate the distribution of each $\mu_{l,\ l \in \{1,\ldots,L\}}$ with a normal distribution:

$$N(E[\mu_l], \sqrt{var[\mu_l]}) = N\left(\frac{\beta_1 + k}{\beta_1 + \beta_2 + n_l}, \sqrt{\frac{(\beta_1 + k)(\beta_2 + n_l - k)}{(\beta_1 + \beta_2 + n_l)^2(\beta_1 + \beta_2 + n_l + 1)}}\right) \tag{3.30}$$

that means, the Beta distribution of each $\mu_{l, l \in \{1,\ldots,L\}}$ is approximated by a normal distribution, which has as a mean $E[\mu_l]$ and standard deviation $\sqrt{var[\mu_l]}$.

Since, from equation (3.5a) the expected mean of the reliability we are estimating, $\hat{R}$, is defined as $E[\widehat{R}] = 1 - \sum_{i=1}^{L} p_i \mu_i$, it follows that we can approximate the distribution of $\hat{R}$ to a normal distribution.

Now, we want to compute based on the failure rate $\mu_{l, l \in \{1,\ldots,L\}}$ and its variance $var[\mu_l] = \sigma_l$, the number of test cases to select optimally from each sub-domain $\mathcal{D}_{l,\quad l \in \{1,\ldots,L\}}$ to meet with the stopping criteria (i.e, stop reliability testing as soon as the reliability is estimated with a confidence level of $1 - \alpha$, with a margin of error d).

Let a_l (as defined in Section 2.5) be the allocation ratio for the sub-domain $\mathcal{D}_l$, with $n_l = n.a_l$ and n the total number of selected test cases defined as $n = \sum_{i=1}^{L} n_l$.

Let z be the upper $\alpha/2$ critical point of the standard normal distribution. Then, we want to find n such that $z[\mathrm{var}[\widehat{R}]]^{1/2} = d$ (margin of error equation), where $\mathrm{var}[\widehat{R}] = \sum_{i=1}^{L} {p_i}^2 \frac{{\sigma_i}^2}{n_i}$ (recall equation (3.5b)).

From equation (2.22), we have $n_l = c^* a_l$ with a_l defined as:

$$a_l = \frac{\sigma_l / \sqrt{c_l}}{\sum_{i=1}^{L} p_i . \sigma_i . \sqrt{c_i}}$$

Consequently, we can rewrite $\text{var}[\widehat{R}]$ as follows:

$$\text{var}[\widehat{R}] = \sum_{i=1}^{L} p_i{}^2 \frac{\sigma_i{}^2}{c^* a_l} \tag{3.31}$$

$$= \frac{1}{c^*} \cdot \sum_{i=1}^{L} p_i{}^2 \frac{\sigma_i{}^2}{a_l} \tag{3.32}$$

Now, we compute the total cost c^* required to reach the desired level of accuracy. By solving the margin of error equation $z[\text{var}[\widehat{R}]]^{1/2} = d$, for c^* and by ignoring the finite population factor as in Section 2.5 we get:

$$c^* = \frac{z^2}{d^2} \left[\sum_{i=1}^{L} p_i . \sigma_i . \sqrt{c_i} \right]^2$$

Having computed both a_l and c^*, we can compute each $n_l = a_l c^*$.

3.10. Adaptive Constrained Statistical Testing

Based on the discussions above, the adaptive constrained statistical testing approach works as described in algorithm 7.

In the initialization phase (lines 1-3), first algorithm 3 is called. Since our approach is based on variance computation of the failure rate in each sub-domain, we require at least 2 test cases pro sub-domain. Based on this requirement, algorithm 3 computes the number of test cases to start with n_{start} (line 2 in algorithm 3). This means that at least 2 test cases should be selected from the sub-domain with the smallest probability of occurrence p_{min}. Having computed n_{start}, the algorithm selects $|\mathcal{T}_{(\mathcal{D}_i, p_i)}|$ test cases from each sub-domain $\mathcal{D}_i$ randomly proportional to its probability p_i (line 4 in algorithm 3). In the second step of the initialization phase (line 2), algorithm 4 is called to compute the failure rate in each sub-domain in the initialization phase. Algorithm 4 initializes the Beta prior of the failure rate of each sub-domain with a non-informative uniform prior, since at the initialization phase we have no information about the failure rate (line 2 in algorithm 4). Then, the $|\mathcal{T}_{(\mathcal{D}_i, p_i)}|$ test cases are executed (line 2 in algorithm 4), and the number of failures are counted (line 4 in algorithm 4). Based on the number of failures k, compute the failure rate $\hat{\mu}_i$ (line 5 in algorithm 4) and its variance ${\sigma_i}^2$ (line 6 in algorithm 4) are computed as proposed in equations (3.28g, 3.29b). $\hat{\mu}_i$ and ${\sigma_i}^2$ are then used to update our Beta prior (lines 7-8 in algorithm 4) as proposed in equations (3.22a, 3.22b).

In the adaptive constrained test selection phase (lines 4-12), algorithm 5 is called to compute the optimal required number of test cases to be select from each sub-domain, based on the stopping criteria formula (lines 3-5 in algorithm 5). Extra test cases are then selected if required (lines 6-8 algorithm 5). Otherwise, test cases have been optimally selected from that sub-domain (line 9 algorithm 5). In the case, when extra test cases should be selected from a sub-domain, the new failure rate $\hat{\mu}_i$ and its variance ${\sigma_i}^2$ (line 9) are computed by calling algorithm 6.

The algorithm stops and returns the estimated reliability if (i) a maximal allowed test time interval Δ has passed or (ii) for all sub-domains the optimal required number of test cases has been selected and the total selected test cases are 100% similar to the operational profile (line 6).

Important Note: for presentation purposes, we illustrate the execution of the selected test cases from each sub-domain in a batch mode. However, in reality the test cases are selected from each sub-domain. Then, the execution is done based on the operational profile as illustrated in Section 2.1.3.

Algorithm 3: computeInitialTestCases

Require: $OP = \{(\mathcal{D}_i, p_i) | i \in \{1, ..., L\}, \sum_{i=1}^{L} p_i = 1\}$

  $p_{min} = min\{p_i | i \in \{1, \ldots, L\}\}$

  $n_{\text{start}} = \frac{2}{p_{min}}$

  for $(\mathcal{D}_i, p_i) \in OP$ **do**

    $|\mathcal{T}_{(\mathcal{D}_i, p_i)}| \leftarrow \lceil n_{\text{start}} \cdot p_i \rceil$

  end for

  return $\mathcal{T}_{OP} = \{\mathcal{T}_{(\mathcal{D}_i, p_i)} | (\mathcal{D}_i, p_i) \in OP\}$

Algorithm 4: computePriorFailureRate

Require:
$\mathcal{T}_{OP} = \{\mathcal{T}_{(\mathcal{D}_i,p_i)} | (\mathcal{D}_i,p_i) \in OP = \{(\mathcal{D}_i,p_i) | i \in \{1,...,L\}, \sum_{i=1}^{L} p_i = 1\}\}$

for $(\mathcal{D}_i,p_i) \in OP$ **do**
  $\beta_1{}^i = \beta_2{}^i = 1$ set uniform prior
  execute the $|\mathcal{T}_{(\mathcal{D}_i,p_i)}|$ test cases
  $k \leftarrow$ number of failures after execution
  $\hat{\mu}_i \leftarrow \frac{1+k}{2+|\mathcal{T}_{(\mathcal{D}_i,p_i)}|}$ see equation (3.28g)
  $\sigma_i{}^2 \leftarrow \frac{(1+k)(1+|\mathcal{T}_{(\mathcal{D}_i,p_i)}|-k)}{(2+|\mathcal{T}_{(\mathcal{D}_i,p_i)}|)^2(3+|\mathcal{T}_{(\mathcal{D}_i,p_i)}|)}$ see equation (3.29b)
  // update prior as proposed in equations (3.22a, 3.22b)
  $\beta_1{}^i \leftarrow \hat{\mu}_i |\mathcal{T}_{(\mathcal{D}_i,p_i)}|$
  $\beta_2{}^i \leftarrow (1-\hat{\mu}_i)|\mathcal{T}_{(\mathcal{D}_i,p_i)}|$
end for
return $OP_{\text{new}} = \{(\mathcal{D}_i,p_i,\hat{\mu}_i,\sigma_i{}^2,\beta_1{}^i,\beta_2{}^i) | i \in \{1,...,L\}\}\}$

Algorithm 5: computeOptimalTestCases

Require: $OP_{\text{new}} = \{(\mathcal{D}_i,p_i,\hat{\mu}_i,\sigma_i{}^2,\beta_1{}^i,\beta_2{}^i)) | i \in \{1,...,L\}\}$
  $opt = 0$
  for $(\mathcal{D}_i,p_i,\hat{\mu}_i,\sigma_i{}^2,\beta_1{}^i,\beta_2{}^i)) \in OP_{\text{new}}$ **do**
    $c^* = \frac{z^2}{d^2}\left[\sum_{i=1}^{L} p_i.\sigma_i.\sqrt{(1-p_i)}\right]^2$
    $a_i = \frac{p_i.\sigma_i/\sqrt{(1-p_i)}}{\sum_{k=1}^{L} p_k.\sigma_k.\sqrt{(1-p_k)}}$
    $n_i^o = \lceil c^* a_i \rceil$
    if $|\mathcal{T}_{(\mathcal{D}_i,p_i)}| < n_i^o$ **then**
      $|\mathcal{T}_{(\mathcal{D}_i,p_i)}| \leftarrow n_i^o$ select extra $(n_i^o - |\mathcal{T}_{(\mathcal{D}_i,p_i)}|)$ test cases from $(\mathcal{D}_i,p_i)$
    else
      opt = opt + 1
    end if
  end for
  Adjust to proportional sampling: call Algorithm 1
  return $(\mathcal{T}_{OP},\ opt)$

Algorithm 6: computePosteriorFailureRate

Require: $OP_{\text{new}} = \{(\mathcal{D}_i, p_i, \hat{\mu}_i, {\sigma_i}^2, {\beta_1}^i, {\beta_2}^i))|i \in \{1, ..., L\}\}$
for $(\mathcal{D}_i, p_i, \hat{\mu}_i, {\sigma_i}^2, {\beta_1}^i, {\beta_2}^i)) \in OP_{\text{new}}$ **do**
execute the $|\mathcal{T}_{(\mathcal{D}_i, p_i)}|$ test cases
$k \leftarrow$ number of failures after execution
//update statistics
$\hat{\mu}_i \leftarrow \frac{{\beta_1}^i + k}{{\beta_1}^i + {\beta_2}^i + |\mathcal{T}_{(\mathcal{D}_i, p_i)}|}$ see equation (3.28g)
${\sigma_i}^2 \leftarrow \frac{({\beta_1}^i + k)({\beta_2}^i + |\mathcal{T}_{(\mathcal{D}_i, p_i)}| - k)}{({\beta_1}^i + {\beta_2}^i + |\mathcal{T}_{(\mathcal{D}_i, p_i)}|)^2({\beta_1}^i + {\beta_2}^i + |\mathcal{T}_{(\mathcal{D}_i, p_i)}| + 1)}$ see equation (3.29b)
end for
return $\{(\mathcal{D}_i, p_i, \hat{\mu}_i, {\sigma_i}^2, {\beta_1}^i, {\beta_2}^i)|i \in \{1, ..., L\}\}$

Algorithm 7: Adaptive constrained statistical testing

Require: $OP = \{(\mathcal{D}_i, p_i)|i \in \{1, ..., L\}, \sum_{i=1}^{L} p_i = 1\}$
Δ : maximal allowed test time
$1 - \alpha$: confidence level
d : margin of error
//1. Initialization
$\mathcal{T}_{OP}$ = computeIntialTestCases(OP)
$\{(\mathcal{D}_i, p_i, \hat{\mu}_i, {\sigma_i}^2, {\beta_1}^i, {\beta_2}^i)|i \in \{1, ..., L\}\}$ = computePriorFailure($\mathcal{T}_{OP}$)
Repair faults if failures are revealed
//2. Adaptive constrained test selection
while true **do**
($\mathcal{T}_{OP}$, opt) = computeOptimalTestCases($\{\{(\mathcal{D}_i, p_i, \hat{\mu}_i, {\sigma_i}^2, {\beta_1}^i, {\beta_2}^i)|i \in \{1, ..., L\}\}\}$)
if Δ passed or (opt $= L \wedge \mathcal{SC}(\mathcal{T}_{OP}) = 100\%$) **then**
break;
end if
$\{(\mathcal{D}_i, p_i, \hat{\mu}_i, {\sigma_i}^2, {\beta_1}^i, {\beta_2}^i)|i \in \{1, ..., L\}\}$ = computePosteriorFailureRate($\mathcal{T}_{OP}$, $\{(\mathcal{D}_i, p_i, \hat{\mu}_i, {\sigma_i}^2, {\beta_1}^i, {\beta_2}^i)|i \in \{1, ..., L\}\}$)
Repair faults
opt = 1
end while
return $\widehat{R} = \sum_{i=1}^{L} p_i.(1 - \hat{\mu}_i)$, $\text{var}[\widehat{R}] = \sum_{i=1}^{L} {p_i}^2 \frac{{\sigma_i}^2}{|\mathcal{T}_{(\mathcal{D}_i, p_i)}|}$

3.11. Predictive Adaptive Constrained Statistical Testing

Algorithm 6 requires at each iteration of the approach the execution of $|\mathcal{T}_{(\mathcal{D}_i,p_i)}|$ test cases. The number of failures after the execution of the test cases as well as the total number of executions are used to build the posterior failure rate for each sub-domain $\mathcal{D}_l$. The posterior is specified by the expected failure rate $\hat{\mu_l}$ and its variance ${\sigma_l}^2$.

Instead of executing the $|\mathcal{T}_{(\mathcal{D}_i,p_i)}|$ test cases for each sub-domain, we propose to predict the failure rate in each sub-domain based on previous test cases executions. The prediction model must be able to predict the failure rate as well as to deliver some measure of uncertainty about the prediction, which is the variance of the estimate.

We model the failure rate in each sub-domain as a Gaussian process distribution. A Gauss process over a univariate real function $f(\mathbf{x})$ [1] is fully specified by its mean function $\mu\mathbf{x}$ and its covariance function $k(\mathbf{x},\mathbf{x}')$. The kernel or covariance function k captures regularity in the form of the correlation of the marginal distributions $f(\mathbf{x})$ and $f(\mathbf{x}')$ [80].

In our failure rate prediction setting, we model the failure rate in each sub-domain $\mathcal{D}_i$ as a Gauss process $f_i(\mathbf{x})$ in function of the number of test cases to be executed, i.e., $|\mathcal{T}_{(\mathcal{D}_i,p_i)}|$.

Each time t the algorithm 6 is called, instead of executing the $|\mathcal{T}_{(\mathcal{D}_i,p_i)}|$ test cases, we make a prediction using the Gaussian process $f_i(\mathbf{x})$. This would yield to:

$$\hat{\mu_i} = f_i(\mathbf{x}) + \epsilon_i$$

After T calls of the algorithm 6, we obtain a vector $\mathbf{y}_{T,i} = \{y_{1,i}, \ldots, y_{T,i}\}$. If we assumen that $\epsilon_i \sim N(0, {\sigma_{in}}^2)$ (i.i.d. Gaussian noise), then the posterior distribution of $f_i(\mathbf{x})$ is a Gaussian process defined by its mean value $\mu_{T,i}(\mathbf{x})$, covariance $k_{T,i}(\mathbf{x},\mathbf{x}')$, and its variance $\sigma^2_{T,i}(\mathbf{x})$ defined as follows [80]:

[1] bold symbols denote vectors

$$\mu_{T,i}(\mathbf{x}) = \mathbf{k}_{T,i}(\mathbf{x})^T(\mathbf{K}_{T,i} + \sigma_{in}{}^2\mathbf{I})^{-1}\mathbf{y}_{T,i}$$

$$k_{T,i}(\mathbf{x}, \mathbf{x}') = k_i(\mathbf{x}, \mathbf{x}') - \mathbf{k}_{T,i}(\mathbf{x})^T(\mathbf{K}_{T,i} + \sigma_{in}{}^2\mathbf{I})^{-1}\mathbf{k}_{T,i}(\mathbf{x}')$$

$$\sigma^2_{T,i}(\mathbf{x}) = k_{T,i}(\mathbf{x}, \mathbf{x})$$

with $\mathbf{x}$ is a number of test cases to be executed from sub-domain $\mathcal{D}_i$, $\mathbf{k}_{T,i}(\mathbf{x}) = (k_i(\mathbf{x}, \mathbf{x}_t))_{1\leq t\leq T}$, and $\mathbf{K}_{T,i} = (k_i(\mathbf{x}_l, \mathbf{x}_m))_{1\leq l,m\leq T}$.

Therefore, the failure rate of sub-domain $\mathcal{D}_i$ can be estimated by:

$$\hat{\mu}_i = \mu_{T,i}(\mathbf{x})$$

and the variance of the estimated failure rate is:

$$\sigma_i{}^2 = \sigma^2_{T,i}(\mathbf{x})$$

Consequently, the posterior Gauss process provides a measure of uncertainty about $f_i(\mathbf{x})$ for test cases that has not been yet executed. We design now our predictive algorithm 8 which is informed by this uncertainty.

In the initialization phase of algorithm 8, the prior computed about the failure rate in each sub-domain (line 2) as well as the number of test cases selected from each sub-domain (line 1) are used to train a Gaussian process for each sub-domain. The algorithm then works the same way as the non-predictive algorithm 7, except in line 13, where the algorithm 9 is called.

In Algorithm 9, for each sub-domain its corresponding Gaussian process f_i is used to predict the failure rate $\hat{\mu}_i$ and get a measure of the uncertainty about the prediction $\sigma_i{}^2$ (lines 2 and 3). Then, the condition in line 4 is verified. The condition sets an upper-bound for the predicted failure rate and its variance based on the formulas used to compute the prior failure rate in lines 7 and 8. Both formulas are parameterized with the variable k representing the number of failures revealed after executing $|\mathcal{T}_{(\mathcal{D}_i,p_i)}|$ test cases. Consequently, the maximal number of possible failures is $k = |\mathcal{T}_{(\mathcal{D}_i,p_i)}|$, which is then used to set upper-bound for both the predicted failure rate and its variance.

Algorithm 8: Predictive adaptive constrained statistical testing

Require: $OP = \{(\mathcal{D}_i, p_i) | i \in \{1, ..., L\}, \sum_{i=1}^{L} p_i = 1\}$
Δ : maximal allowed test time
$1 - \alpha$: confidence level
d : margin of error
//1. Initialization
$\mathcal{T}_{OP}$ = computeIntialTestCases(OP)
$\{(\mathcal{D}_i, p_i, \hat{\mu}_i, {\sigma_i}^2, {\beta_1}^i, {\beta_2}^i) | i \in \{1, ..., L\}\}$ =
computePriorFailureRate($\mathcal{T}_{OP}$)
$t = 0$ //Gaussian process training
for $(\hat{\mu}_i, |\mathcal{T}_{(\mathcal{D}_i, p_i)}|)$ **do**
5: train Gaussian process $f_i(|\mathcal{T}_{(\mathcal{D}_i, p_i)}|)$
end for
Repair faults if failures are revealed
//2. Adaptive constrained test selection
while true **do**
($\mathcal{T}_{OP}$, opt) = computeOptimalTestCases($\{(\mathcal{D}_i, p_i, \hat{\mu}_i, {\sigma_i}^2, {\beta_1}^i, {\beta_2}^i) | i \in \{1, ..., L\}\}$)
10: **if** Δ passed or (opt $= L \wedge \mathcal{SC}(\mathcal{T}_{OP}) = 100\%$) **then**
break;
end if
$\{(\mathcal{D}_i, p_i, \hat{\mu}_i, {\sigma_i}^2, {\beta_1}^i, {\beta_2}^i) | i \in \{1, ..., L\}\}$ =
computeOrPredictPosteriorFailureRate($\mathcal{T}_{OP}$, $\{(\mathcal{D}_i, p_i, \hat{\mu}_i, {\sigma_i}^2, {\beta_1}^i, {\beta_2}^i) | i \in \{1, ..., L\}\}$)
Repair faults
15: opt = 1
$t = t + 1$
end while
return $\widehat{R} = \sum_{i=1}^{L} p_i.(1 - \hat{\mu}_i)$, $\text{var}[\widehat{R}] = \sum_{i=1}^{L} {p_i}^2 \frac{{\sigma_i}^2}{|\mathcal{T}_{(\mathcal{D}_i, p_i)}|}$

If the prediction of the Gaussian process f_i is judged unrealistic, based on the condition in line 4, then the $|\mathcal{T}_{(\mathcal{D}_i, p_i)}|$ are executed and the Gaussian process is trained with the computed posterior (line alg:TrainAgain).

Many researches are showing that software faults can be well predicted using software metrics (e.g., [36], [49], or [55]). Consequently, if such metrics are available it would make sense to model them as independent variables (in addition to the number of test cases) in the Gaussian process f_i of the failure rate. In Section 6.1.2, we show experimentally that considering software metrics can indeed increase the accuracy of our prediction model.

Algorithm 9: computeOrPredictPosteriorFailureRate

Require: $OP_{\text{new}} = \{(\mathcal{D}_i, p_i, \hat{\mu}_i, {\sigma_i}^2, {\beta_1}^i, {\beta_2}^i))|i \in \{1, ..., L\}\}$

for $(\mathcal{D}_i, p_i, \hat{\mu}_i, {\sigma_i}^2, {\beta_1}^i, {\beta_2}^i)) \in OP_{\text{new}}$ **do**

$\hat{\mu}_i \leftarrow \mu_{t,i}(|\mathcal{T}_{(\mathcal{D}_i,p_i)}|)$

${\sigma_i}^2 \leftarrow {\sigma_{t,i}}^2(|\mathcal{T}_{(\mathcal{D}_i,p_i)}|)$

if $\neg(({\sigma_i}^2 < \frac{({\beta_1}^i+|\mathcal{T}_{(\mathcal{D}_i,p_i)}|){\beta_2}^i}{({\beta_1}^i+{\beta_2}^i+|\mathcal{T}_{(\mathcal{D}_i,p_i)}|)^2({\beta_1}^i+{\beta_2}^i+|\mathcal{T}_{(\mathcal{D}_i,p_i)}|+1)}) \wedge (\hat{\mu}_i < \frac{{\beta_1}^i+|\mathcal{T}_{(\mathcal{D}_i,p_i)}|}{{\beta_1}^i+{\beta_2}^i+|\mathcal{T}_{(\mathcal{D}_i,p_i)}|}))$ **then**

execute the $|\mathcal{T}_{(\mathcal{D}_i,p_i)}|$ test cases

$k \leftarrow$ number of failures after execution

//update statistics

$\hat{\mu}_i \leftarrow \frac{{\beta_1}^i+k}{{\beta_1}^i+{\beta_2}^i+|\mathcal{T}_{(\mathcal{D}_i,p_i)}|}$ see equation (3.28g)

${\sigma_i}^2 \leftarrow \frac{({\beta_1}^i+k)({\beta_2}^i+|\mathcal{T}_{(\mathcal{D}_i,p_i)}|-k)}{({\beta_1}^i+{\beta_2}^i+|\mathcal{T}_{(\mathcal{D}_i,p_i)}|)^2({\beta_1}^i+{\beta_2}^i+|\mathcal{T}_{(\mathcal{D}_i,p_i)}|+1)}$ see equation (3.29b)

train Gaussian process f_i with the new independent variable $|\mathcal{T}_{(\mathcal{D}_i,p_i)}|$ and the new dependent variable ${\sigma_i}^2$

end if

end for

return $\{(\mathcal{D}_i, p_i, \hat{\mu}_i, {\sigma_i}^2, {\beta_1}^i, {\beta_2}^i)|i \in \{1, ..., L\}\}$

3.12. Asymptotic Analysis

In the following, we prove the termination of algorithm 7, when Δ (maximal allowed test time) is set to $\Delta = \infty$.

We also prove that our algorithm asymptotically converges to optimal stratified sampling.

Theorem 3.1. *The adaptive constrained test selection algorithm terminates with probability one, if* $\Delta = \infty$

Proof. Let μ_l, be the true failure rate of a sub-domain $\mathcal{D}_l$ ($l \in \{1, \ldots, L\}$). Assume, that n_l test cases are selected from $\mathcal{D}_l$ and the test cases has the outcome $X_{1,l}, \ldots, X_{n_l,l}$. Suppose that k failures are observed, meaning $\sum_{i=1}^{n_l} X_{i,l} = k$.

Now, let $\beta_1 > 0$ and $\beta_2 > 0$ be the parameters of the Beta prior of the estimate $\hat{\mu}_l$ of μ_l. From equation (3.28g), we know that:

$$\hat{\mu}_l = E[\mu_l] = \frac{\beta_1 + k}{\beta_1 + \beta_2 + n_l}$$

and:

$$\sigma_l{}^2 = var[\mu_l] = E[(\mu_l - \hat{\mu}_l)^2] = \frac{(\beta_1 + k)(\beta_2 + n_l - k)}{(\beta_1 + \beta_2 + n_l)^2(\beta_1 + \beta_2 + n_l + 1)}$$

Since $k \leq n_l$ and $\beta_1 > 0$ and $\beta_2 > 0$ it follows:

$$\begin{aligned} \sigma_l{}^2 &\leq \frac{(n_l + \beta_1)\beta_2}{\beta_1 + \beta_2 + n_l)^2(\beta_1 + \beta_2 + n_l + 1)} \\ &\leq \frac{(n_l + \beta_1 + \beta_2)(\beta_2 + \beta_1 + 1 + n_l)}{(\beta_1 + \beta_2 + n_l)^2(\beta_1 + \beta_2 + n_l + 1)} \\ &= \frac{1}{\beta_1 + \beta_2 + n_l} \end{aligned}$$

Consequently, it follows:

$$\lim_{n_l \to \infty} \sigma_l{}^2 = 0 \tag{3.34}$$

This means, that the posterior variance of the failure rate tend to be 0 as we execute more test cases from sub-domain $\mathcal{D}_i$.

Therefore, since both β_1 and β_2 are fix, we can conclude from the law of large numbers that:

$$\lim_{n_l \to \infty} \hat{\mu}_l = \mu_l \tag{3.35}$$

that is, $\hat{\mu}_l$ converges almost surely to the true failure rate μ_l.

Since our algorithm returns a confidence interval which contains μ_l with a posterior probability of at least $1 - \alpha$ and margin of error d (i.e., it means the confidence interval has a width $2d$), it follows from equation (3.35), that the posterior probability $\mathbb{P}(\hat{\mu}_l - d \leq \mu_l \leq \hat{\mu}_l + d)$ must converge almost surely to 1 as $n_l \longrightarrow \infty$.

□

Theorem 3.2. *The adaptive constrained test selection algorithm converges asymptotically to optimal stratified sampling*

Proof. Our approach adjusts the test allocation at each iteration to 100% similarity to the operational profile, which means that our approach is in fact a proportional stratified sampling.

From theorem 3.1, we proved in equation (3.34) that the variance of the failure rate of each sub-domain $\mathcal{D}_l$ converges to 0 as $n_l \longrightarrow \infty$. This means, that asymptotically, the standard deviations of the failure rate in all sub-domains are all equal, more precisely equal to 0. According to theorem 2.2, it follows that our sampling scheme converges asymptotically to optimal stratified sampling.

□

3.13. Discussion

After each iteration of our approach, if failures are revealed, then the responsible faults are repaired. Therefore, one could argue that after repairing the faults the failure rate is expected to decrease. However, our approach assumes that the failure rate remains the same after fault repair. We defend our decision on the ground that there is no quantifiable measure of the contribution of individual faults to the failure rate of the software as proposed by [58].

However, our approach does not consider the case when a fault repair introduces new faults and hence increases the failure rate. In order to address such a limitation, a model for fault-repair operation may be needed to account for erroneous fault repairs. The development of such a model can be considered as a future work.

4. Adaptive Constrained Weighted White-Box Statistical Testing

In this Chapter, we consider the case where in addition to the operational profile of the software component under study, we have access to the source code implementing the component. Our goal is to make use of the information provided by the source code to enhance the black-box approach presented in Chapter 3 by further reducing the number of test cases to be executed to reach a required statistical confidence on the reliability estimate.

Before introducing our approach, it is necessary to introduce the following terms. we differentiate between two type of faults [96]: (i) domain faults, and (ii) computation faults. Domain faults are faults in the control flow of the program, which cause the execution of the wrong program paths for some inputs because they create a shift in the input boundaries of the the program path. Computation faults are faults that cause the wrong computation of a function for one or more inputs.

4.1. Problem Definition

The black-box approach we developed in Chapter 3 is based on the principle of optimal stratified sampling. The goal of optimal stratified sampling is to decrease the variance of the failure rate within each sub-domain to decrease the overall variance of the reliability estimator. This can be illustrated using the Anova (Analysis of variance) principle as follows:

$var(\text{total}) = var(\text{within sub-domains}) + var(\text{between sub-domains})$

Since per construction, the operational profile sub-domains are disjoints, and since we assume that the test cases outputs are independent (assumption 2 in Section 3.4), then it follows $var(\text{between sub-domains}) = 0$.

Consequently, the goal of the black-box approach we presented in Chapter 3 is to reduce the variance of the failure rate within each sub-domain of the operational profile.

If, we could reduce the variance of the failure rate in each sub-domain we could reduce the required test cases to execute from each sub-domain. More precisely, if the sub-domains were homogeneous, then we would require to execute only one test case from each sub-domain.

Different studies has been conducted to compare the performance of random testing and partition testing ([33], [94]), where the results were conform to the theory of stratified sampling (see Section 2.5). The results confirm that for the same testing effort, partition testing is more cost effective than random sampling only if proportional sampling is used. Furthermore, if the partitions are homogeneous then the number of test cases required by partition testing will be significantly reduced compared to random sampling (since only one test case is needed for each partition). However, homogeneous partitions of the input domain are very difficult to obtain in practice, as we show in Section 4.2.

We present in the following an approach to transform the given operational profile sub-domains in fine-grained ones by using the information provided by the source code. The goal is to define new sub-domains which are more or less homogeneous. These sub-domains will be then used to generate statistical test cases to assess the reliability of the software under study. We compute for each of the new defined sub-domains a probability. This probability weigh the contribution of each test case execution on the overall reliability estimate.

4.2. Research Goals

The failure rate of a software program when executed with inputs from a sub-domain $\mathcal{D}_{i,\ i\in\{1,\ldots,L\}}$ is the failure rate of the possible program executions induced by the inputs of $\mathcal{D}_{i,\ i\in\{1,\ldots,L\}}$. It would be ideal if we could separate successful program execution from the failing ones. However, this is not likely, as explained in Section 3.1.

A program execution is a program path executed with an input value from the program's input domain. A program path is a sequence of statements, and each program path defines an equivalence class on the input values which can execute it. Consequently, the failure rate of the program when executed with inputs from $\mathcal{D}_{i,\ i \in \{1,\ldots,L\}}$ is the failure rate of the possible program paths when executed with inputs from that sub-domain.

We propose the stratification of each sub-domain $\mathcal{D}_{i,\ i \in \{1,\ldots,L\}}$ into partitions of inputs, where each partition executes a program path (i.e., similar program executions). Each partition (i.e., strata) is then a program path.

Symbolic execution (definition can be found in Section 2.8) is a technique for grouping program inputs which produce the same symbolic output. The output of symbolic execution is a set of path conditions. A path condition is a set of constraints on the program inputs. The satisfaction of the constraints lead to the execution of the program path represented by the path condition. If we assume that the symbolic execution of a program always terminates (we will relax this assumption in Section 4.8), then all path conditions define a complete partition of the input domain. Therefore, the path conditions define the strata of our stratification scheme. The inputs which satisfy a path condition lead to the execution of the corresponding program path.

The inputs satisfying a path condition are not necessarily homogeneous. If the program path contains some faults, then some inputs would still execute failure-free. For example the shifts caused by domain faults can be very small, then most of the inputs would execute failure-free. Furthermore, arithmetic overflow failures are data-dependent which would contradict with homogeneity assumption of the path conditions.

[96] proposed a technique to detect domain faults. The technique generates test inputs in the boundaries of the input domain of each program path to detect possible shifts. However, it is difficult and impractical to determine the input domain boundaries of each program path, which would require among other thing the exhaustive counting of all inputs satisfying the path condition representing the program path. A practical alternative to the above technique is to randomly execute inputs for each program path to increase the probability of revealing both domain faults and computation errors.

Consequently, since the inputs executing a program path are not truly homogeneous, then more than a test case pro program path is required. The important question that arises is for each path condition, how many input values which satisfy that path condition should be selected?

Furthermore, the program paths induced by the path conditions are not equally likely to be executed when the program is executed according to the operational profile. Consequently, the next question that arises is: which program paths are likely to be executed and how probable is the execution of each program path?

The goal of this Chapter is to present an approach to compute the probability of execution of a path condition given an operational profile, which is the answer for the second question.

The fist question is answered by using our black-box approach we presented in Chapter 3. We give the black-box approach as input the program path conditions together with their probability of execution as the new sub-domains of the original operational profile.

We have published part of the following results in [73].

4.3. Assumptions

We adopt the same assumptions as in Section 3.4, with the following exceptions:

- We relax assumption 5 in 3.4 as follows: we assume that failures are uniformly distributed over the program paths.
- We assume that the input domain of the software under study is finite.

4.4. Motivating Example and Challenges

Consider the code in Figure 4.1. Assume we want to estimate the probability of not reaching line 9, where an exception can arise. Assume the input variables x and y range over the integer domain [1...100]. The input domain has then $10^2 \times 10^2 = 10^4$ possible input values.

```
1 void method(int x, int y) {
2   if(y == x*10)
3     S0;
4   else
5     S1;
6   if(x > 5 && y > 10)
7     S2;
8   else
9     assert false;
10 }
```

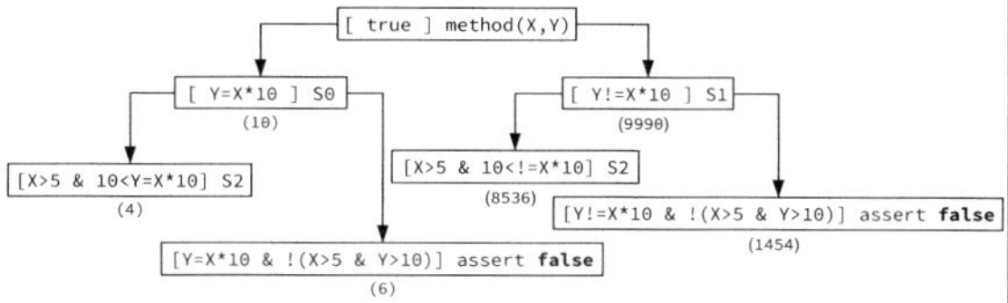

Figure 4.1.: Illustrative example and its symbolic execution tree

Consider the symbolic execution tree in Figure 4.1. Each node in the tree is a branching constraint over the program inputs.

Assume now, that we want to compute the probability of executing the statement assert false at line 9. The are two path conditions which would execute line 9:

1. $PC_1 = Y = X * 10\&![X > 5\&Y > 10]$
2. $PC_2 = Y =!X * 10\&![X > 5\&Y > 10]$

where ! stands for the logical not.

If we assume that the inputs are uniformly distributed within the input domain, then the probability of line 9 is:

$$\mathbb{P}(line\ 9) = \mathbb{P}(PC_1) + \mathbb{P}(PC_2)$$

The probability of executing PC_1, is defined as:

$$\mathbb{P}(PC_1) = \frac{\#\text{(x,y) satisfying } PC_1 \text{ given that } x \in [1, 100] \text{ and } y \in [1, 100]}{\text{cardinality of the input domain}}$$

$$= \frac{\text{cardinality of the solution space of } PC_1 \text{ given the defintion domain}}{\text{cardinality of the input domain}}$$

Since the constraints in the program in Figure 4.1 are all linear, we can use model counting, to count for each constraint the number of values from the input domain that satisfy that constraint (the counter is in bracket under each constraint). Based on the counting result of the solution space of each constraint we can compute $\mathbb{P}(line\ 9)$:

$$\mathbb{P}(line\ 9) = \frac{6}{10000} + \frac{1454}{10000} = 0.146$$

However, when the path constraints are not linear (e.g, contain cosine, sine functions, etc,.), then model counting cannot be used. In the following, we motivate our idea in computing the solution space of path conditions even if it contains non-linear constraints.

4.4.1. Constraints Solution Space Computation

When solving a constrained problem, one is usually interested in finding one solution or assessing that there is no solution at all. However, knowing the number of solutions can give a new perspective on the constrained problem. In mathematics, a set of linear inequalities form a bounded geometric object. A solution to the set of inequalities is one point in the geometric object. The number of possible solutions is the volume of the geometric object. In the context of program analysis, each path condition is represented as a Boolean combination of constraints. Knowing the volumes of the path conditions allows to compute the probability of executing each path condition.

4.4.2. Interval Branch-and-Prune Algorithms

Consider a vector $\mathbf{x} = (x_1, \ldots, x_n) \in \mathbb{R}^n$ of unknowns. A constrained problem is defined by a set $\mathcal{C} = \{c_1, \ldots, c_l\}$ of l constraints and a bounded domain $\mathcal{D}_\mathbf{x} = \mathcal{D}_{x_1} \times \ldots \times \mathcal{D}_{x_n}$ where $x_k \in \mathcal{D}_{x_k} := \{r \in \mathbb{R} | a_k \leq r \leq b_k\}, k = 1, \ldots, n$.

The solution set of the constrained problem, defined by the constrains set $\mathcal{C}$, is the set of tuples from $\mathbf{x}$ that satisfy all the constraints in $\mathcal{C}$. Counting the solution set of a constrained problem defined over continuous domains involves computing an integral over the geometric object formed by the constraints. However, the constraints may contain nonlinear expressions which can be not differentiable. For this reason, the solution set can be approximated using interval analysis techniques such as Interval Branch-and-Prune algorithms [48]. Interval Branch-and-Prune algorithms generate a set of $n-$dimensional boxes whose union define the solution set of a constrained problem. Such algorithms alternates iterativ branch and prune tasks to generate boxes from the initial bounded domain defined by the Cartesian product $\mathcal{D}_{\mathbf{x}}$. The algorithm stops when a fixed precision is reached. The pruning task eliminates *inconsistent* values and hence reduces the size of a box. The branch task splits the box into smaller boxes [48].

4.5. Overview of the Approach

Figure 4.2 depicts the approach for the adaptive white-box statistical testing. The approach takes as input (i) the source code of the software program, (ii) the expected operational profile and (iii) the reliability assessment goals (i.e, required confidence on the reliability estimate). The approach is based on the ability to execute the source code symbolically. Symbolic execution outputs a set of path conditions. We present in Section 4.8 an extension of symbolic execution, which is probabilistic. The probabilistic symbolic execution gets as input (i) the source code, and (ii) a probabilistic bound. The probabilistic bound is a replacement for the static bound usually set in the context of bounded symbolic execution to limit the symbolic search. The goal of the bound is to avoid the problem of path explosion in the presence of looping constructs. In contrast to state-of-the-art symbolic execution approaches, we control the symbolic execution using a probabilistic bound and not a static one which has no quantitative relation to the reliability estimation goal. The probabilistic bound is incrementally updated and is computed based on the reliability assessment goals. During the symbolic execution of the code, the approach computes the probability of executing each path condition in a compositional manner as shown in Sections 4.6 and 4.7.

The first iteration of the approach starts with the adaptive constrained black-box statistical testing, which we presented in Chapter 3. If the stopping criteria as defined in Section 3.9 is not reached, then this means that failures are revealed. Consequently, the responsible faults should be repaired.

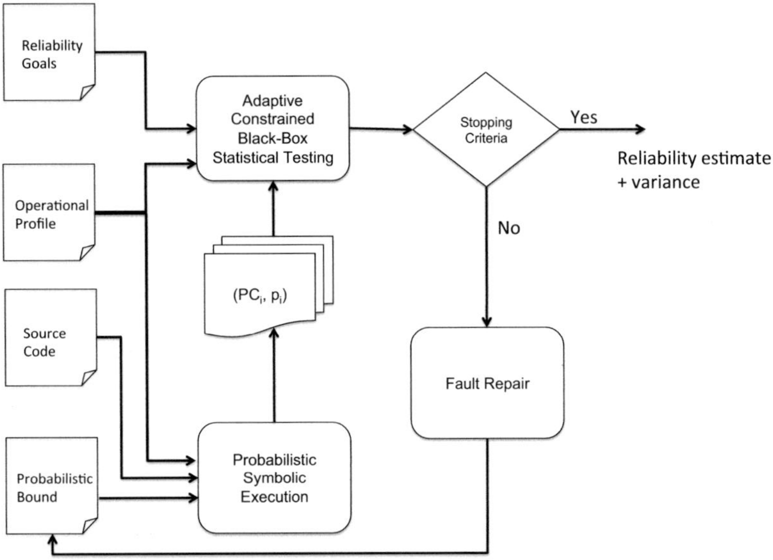

Figure 4.2.: Adaptive Constrained White-Box Statistical Testing

The adaptive constrained black-box statistical testing approach computes then the required number of test cases to be further executed. Based on this number, we compute a probabilistic bound. The probabilistic symbolic execution uses then the probabilistic bound and the source code to compute the probability of occurrence of the path conditions. The set of (PC_i, p_i) is then the new operational profile, which will used in the next iterations by adaptive constrained black-box statistical testing. The approach iterates until the stopping criteria is reached.

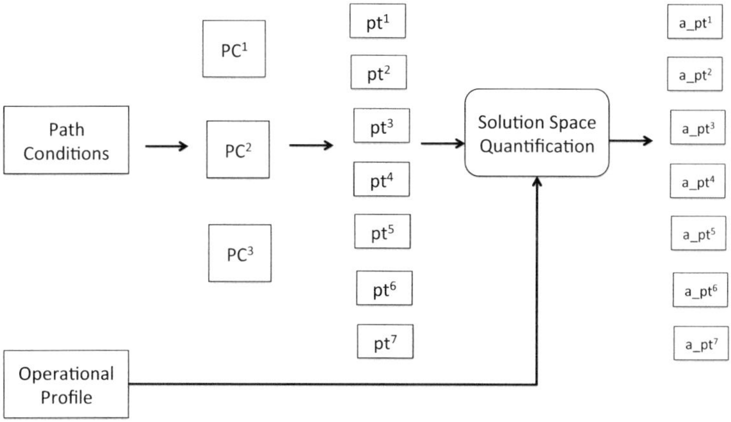

Figure 4.3.: Compositional Solution Space - Divide

In real world programs, the path conditions can very large. Consequently, the quantification of their solution space can be very expensive. We propose a compositional approach to compute the probability of executing each path condition based on the divide and conquer principle as depicted in Figures 4.3 and 4.4. In the divide step in figure 4.3, the path conditions are splitted into a set of variable-independent constraints. The solution space quantification is then executed on each split. In the conquer step in figure 4.4, the approximations of the splits are merged to compute the probability of each path condition in a compositional manner.

4.6. Compositional Path Condition Solution Space Computation

We consider the problem of efficiently computing the solution space of an individual path condition. A path condition is a conjunction of a set of branching constraints. In real world applications, a path condition can be very large (i.e., include a large number of branching constraints). We propose to split a path condition into disjoint sets of branching constraints whose solution space can be determined independently from each other.

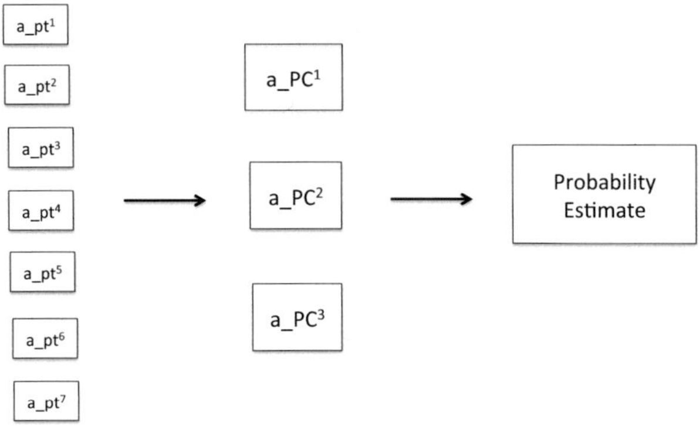

Figure 4.4.: Compositional Solution Space - Conquer

Each branching constraint defines a relation between its variables. Each variable has a definition domain. A constraint ranges over a given definition domain and specifies which values from the domain of its variables are compatible to the relation. More formally, we introduce the following definitions.

Definition 4.1. *(Branching Constraint). A branching constraint c is a triple* $<\mathcal{V}_c, \mathcal{B}_c, \mathcal{R}_c>$*, where* $\mathcal{V}_c$ *is a set of l variables* $<v_1, v_2, \ldots, v_l>$*,* $\mathcal{B}_c$ *is the Cartesian product* $I_1 \times I_2, \ldots \times I_n$ *with* I_k *the definition domain of variable* v_k*, and* $\mathcal{R}_c$ *the constraint relation defined as:*
$\mathcal{R}_c \subseteq \{<i_1, i_2, \ldots i_l>| i_1 \in I_1, i_2 \in I_2, \ldots, i_l \in I_l\}$
$\mathcal{R}_c$ *is a subset of the Cartesian product* $I_1 \times I_2, \ldots I_l$ *with* I_k *the definition domain of variable* v_k *and* i_k *a possible value for variable* v_k*.*

The definition of a path condition follows from the definition of a branching condition as follows:

Definition 4.2. *(Path Condition). A path condition* Φ *is a triple* $<\mathcal{V}_\Phi, \mathcal{B}_\Phi, \mathcal{C}_\Phi>$ *where* $\mathcal{V}_\Phi$ *is a set of n variables* $<v_1, v_2, \ldots, v_n>$*,* $\mathcal{B}_\Phi$ *(a box) the Cartesian product* $I_1 \times I_2, \ldots \times I_n$ *of the variables definition domains where each variable* v_i *ranges over the interval* I_i*, and* $\mathcal{C}_\Phi$ *is a finite set of branching constraints expressed as linear or nonlinear equations or inequalities on subsets of the variables* $\mathcal{V}$*. Consequently, a path condition can be defined as* $\Phi = \bigwedge_{c_i \in \mathcal{C}_\Phi} c_i = <\mathcal{V}_\Phi, \mathcal{B}_\Phi, \mathcal{C}_\Phi>$*.*

Now we move to the definition of the solution space of a path condition. We start with defining a solution to a branching constraint:

Lemma 4.1. *(Branching Constraint Solution). A solution of a branching constraint* $c = <\mathcal{V}_c, \mathcal{B}_c, \mathcal{R}_c>$*, is a tuple* $s_c \in \mathcal{R}_c$ *where* $s_c \subseteq \mathcal{B}_c$*.*

Our ultimate goal is to characterize the complete set of solutions:

Lemma 4.2. *(Branching Constraint Solution Space). The solution space of a branching constraint* $c = <\mathcal{V}_c, \mathcal{B}_c, \mathcal{R}_c>$*, is a set of tuples* $\mathcal{S}_c \subseteq \mathcal{B}_c$ *where:*

- $\forall\, s \in \mathcal{S}_c : s \in \mathcal{R}_c$ *(only solutions inside the set)*
- $\forall_{b \in \mathcal{B}_c} b \notin \mathcal{S}_c : b \notin \mathcal{R}_c$ *(no solutions outside the solution space)*

We propose to split a path condition into a set of disjoint branching constraints that have input variables in common. We define dependent constraints as follows:

Definition 4.3. *(Dependent Branching Constraints). Two branching constraints* $c_i = <\mathcal{V}_{c_i}, \mathcal{B}_{c_i}, \mathcal{R}_{c_i}>$ *and* $c_k = <\mathcal{V}_{c_k}, \mathcal{B}_{c_i}, \mathcal{R}_{c_k}>$ *are called dependent if:* $\mathcal{V}_{c_i} \cap \mathcal{V}_{c_k} \neq \emptyset$*.*

We introduce now a dependency relation among the constraints of a path condition:

Definition 4.4. *(Constraint Dependence Relation). The constraint dependence relation* $\mathcal{DEP} : \mathcal{C} \times \mathcal{C} \longrightarrow Boolean$*, where* $\mathcal{C}$ *a set of constraints, is recursively defined as follows:*

- $\forall c \in \mathcal{C} : \mathcal{DEP}(c, c) = true$
- $\forall c_i, c_j \in \mathcal{C}$, *if* $\mathcal{V}_{c_i} \cap \mathcal{V}_{c_k} \neq \emptyset$, *then* $\mathcal{DEP}(c_i, c_j) = true$
- $\forall c_i, c_j, c_k \in \mathcal{C}$, *if* $\mathcal{DEP}(c_i, c_j) = true \wedge \mathcal{DEP}(c_j, c_k) = true$, *then* $\mathcal{DEP}(c_i, c_k) = true$

Intuitively, two constraints are dependent if they share at least one input variable.

Lemma 4.3. *(Independent Branching Constraint Solution Space). The solution space of the conjunction of two independent branching constraints c_i and c_j is $S_{(c_i \wedge c_j)} = \mathcal{S}_{c_i} \cup \mathcal{S}_{c_j}$.*

The dependency relation allows us to split a path condition in a set of disjoint sets containing independent constraints.

Definition 4.5. *(Path Condition Split). We can split the formula of a path condition $\Phi = \bigwedge_{c_i \in C} c_i = <\mathcal{V}_\Phi, \mathcal{B}_\Phi, \mathcal{C}_\Phi>$ into mutually exclusive and collectively exhaustive sets of constraints (or sub-formulas) based on the constraint dependence relation $\mathcal{DEP}$ as follows:*

- $\mathcal{C}_\Phi = \cup_{i \in \{1,\ldots,m\}} C_i^s$
- *For $i \neq j$, the sets C_i^s and C_j^s are disjoint: $C_i^s \wedge C_j^s = \emptyset$.*
- $\forall c_i, c_j \in C_k^s$: $\mathcal{DEP}(c_i, c_j) = true$
- $\forall c_i \in C_i^s$ *and* $\forall c_j \in C_j^s$: $\mathcal{DEP}(c_i, c_j) = false$

The splitted path condition Φ is defined then as: $\Phi_{split} = \Phi_1 \wedge \Phi_2 \wedge \ldots \wedge \Phi_m$, where $\Phi_i = \bigwedge_{c_k \in C_i^s} c_k = <\mathcal{V}_{\Phi_i}, \mathcal{B}_{\Phi_i}, C_i^s>$.

Note that the dependency relation (see Def. 4.4) is by construction an equivalence relation over the set of constraints. Note also that for two independent constraints c_1 and c_2, the satisfaction of c_1 is independent from the satisfaction of c_2. Additionally, for two independent constraint sets $\mathcal{C}_1$ and $\mathcal{C}_2$, the satisfaction of the constraints in $\mathcal{C}_1$ is independent form the satisfaction of the constraints in $\mathcal{C}_2$.

Lemma 4.4. *(Path Condition Solution Space). The solution space of a path condition $\Phi = \bigwedge_{c_i \in C} c_i = <\mathcal{V}_\Phi, \mathcal{B}_\Phi, \mathcal{C}_\Phi>$ is a set of tuples $\mathcal{S}_\Phi \subseteq \mathcal{B}_\Phi$ where:*

- $\forall_{\mathcal{S} \in \mathcal{S}_\Phi} \forall_{s \in \mathcal{S}} \forall c \in \mathcal{C} : s \in \mathcal{R}_c$ *(only solutions for all path constraints inside the set)*
- $\forall_{\mathcal{B} \subset \mathcal{B}_c} \mathcal{B} \not\subset \mathcal{S}_\Phi : \exists_{b \in \mathcal{B}}\, b \notin \mathcal{R}_c$ *(no solutions outside the solution space)*
- $\mathcal{S}_\Phi = \mathcal{S}_{\Phi_{split}} = \cup_{i \in \{1,\ldots,m\}} \mathcal{S}_{\Phi_i}$

Remarks. The composition of the solution space of a path condition allows us to split the quantification of the solution space of a large path condition into the analysis of smaller and simpler constraints. This allows to parallelize the quantification procedure of the solution space. It also allows us to reuse already quantified constraints (i.e., caching).

4.6.1. Solution Space of Constraints over Finite Floating Domains

We consider now the problem of counting the solution space of constraints defined over finite floating domains. Counting the solution set of constraints defined over continuous domains involves computing an integral over the geometric object formed by the constraints. However, the constraints may contain nonlinear expression which are not differentiable. For this reason, we approximate the solution space of a conjunction of dependent constraints with a set of boxes that cover the exact solutions of the constraints. The union of the boxes is an over-approximation of the solution space but never an under-approximation.

The boxes representing the solution space are extracted using constraint propagation techniques [67]. Constraint propagation techniques implement local reasoning on constraints to eliminate inconsistent values from the definition domains of the constraints variables. Such techniques prune and subdivide the definition domain of the constraints until a stopping criteria is satisfied. Note that the definition domain of the constraints as a Cartesian product of intervals is a set of boxes (See Def. 4.2 and Def. 4.1). The following definitions are adapted from [67], [10] and [9].

Definition 4.6. *(Consistency). A set $\mathcal{B} \subseteq \mathcal{B}_\Phi$ is consistent with a path condition $\Phi = \bigwedge_{c_i \in C} c_i = <\mathcal{V}_\Phi, \mathcal{B}_\Phi, \mathcal{C}_\Phi>$ iff it contains at least one solution of Φ. Otherwise, it is called inconsistent.*

In order to eliminate input values that do not satisfy a constraint, a projection function is associated with each constraint:

Definition 4.7. *(Projection Function). For a path condition* $\Phi = \bigwedge_{c_i \in C} c_i = <\mathcal{V}_\Phi, \mathcal{B}_\Phi, \mathcal{C}_\Phi>$*, a projection* π_c *of a constraint* $c \in \mathcal{C}_\Phi$ *with a solution space* $\mathcal{S}_c$*, is a mapping between the subsets of* $\mathcal{B}_\Phi$ *where* $\forall \mathcal{B} \subset \mathcal{B}_\Phi$*:*

- $\pi_c(\mathcal{B}) \subseteq \mathcal{B}$
- $\forall_{b \in \mathcal{B}}\, b \notin \pi_c(\mathcal{B}) : b \notin \mathcal{S}_c$

Usually the implementation of projection functions relies on interval analysis methods (e.g., the interval newton method). The set of projection functions associated with the constraints are then used to eliminate values from the definition domain that do not satisfy the constraints. The pruning of a box is done using constraint propagation. When a projection function eliminates a value of a variable, this information is propagated to the other constraints depending on that variable. This process terminates when the projection functions cannot further eliminate values (i.e. cannot further reduce the size of the boxes).

Definition 4.8. *(Constraint Propagation). For a path condition* $\Phi = \bigwedge_{c_i \in C} c_i = <\mathcal{V}_\Phi, \mathcal{B}_\Phi, \mathcal{C}_\Phi>$*, let* $\pi_{\mathcal{C}_\Phi}$ *be the set of projections for all the constraints* $\mathcal{C}_\Phi$*. Constraint propagation* $\mathcal{CP}$ *defines a mapping between the the subsets of* $\mathcal{B}_\Phi$ *where* $\forall \mathcal{B} \subset \mathcal{B}_\Phi$*:*

- $\mathcal{CP}(\mathcal{B}) \subseteq \mathcal{B}$ *(contractance)*
- $\forall_{b \in \mathcal{B}}\, b \notin \mathcal{CP}(\mathcal{B}) : \exists c \in \mathcal{C}_\Phi\, b \notin \mathcal{S}_c$ *(correctness)*
- $\forall_{\pi \in \pi_{\mathcal{C}_\Phi}}\, \pi(\mathcal{CP}(\mathcal{B})) = \mathcal{CP}(\mathcal{B})$ *(fixed point)*

The pruning level we can achieve using constraint propagation is dependent on the ability of the projection function to identify value combinations that do not satisfy the analyzed constraint [9]. However, projection functions do not miss any solution [9]. In order to further prune the result boxes, the boxes are subdivided and constraint propagation is applied to each sub-box. Such algorithms are called branch-and-prune algorithms. Such algorithms terminate when for example the box is judged too small to be considered for branching.

Constraint reasoning techniques do not loose any solution during the process of approximating the solution space of a set of constraints. Consequently, using such techniques, we get a safe enclosure for the solution space of a constraint.

Constraint reasoning techniques maintain two coverings for the solution space $\mathcal{S}_\Phi$ of path condition Φ. We assume that the variables $\mathcal{V}_\Phi$ are defined over $\mathbb{R}$, i.e., $\mathcal{B}_\Phi \subseteq \mathbb{R}^{|\mathcal{V}_\Phi|}$

Definition 4.9. *(Outer Box Cover). An outer box cover of $\mathcal{S}_\Phi$ is a set of disjoint boxes $\mathcal{S}_\Phi^\square = \{B_1, \ldots, B_n\}$ where:*

- $\forall_{i \in \{1,\ldots,n\}} B_i \subseteq \mathcal{B}_\Phi \wedge vol(B_i) > 0$
- $\forall_{i,j \in \{1,\ldots,n\} \wedge i \neq j}\ vol(B_i \cap B_j) = 0$
- $\mathcal{S}_\Phi \subseteq \bigcup_{i=1}^{n} B_i$

vol(B_i) is computed as the product of the intervals forming the box B_i.

Complementary to the concept of outer box cover, we define the concept of inner box cover.

Definition 4.10. *(Inner Box Cover). An inner box cover of $\mathcal{S}_\Phi$ is a set of disjoint boxes $\mathcal{S}_\Phi^\blacksquare = \{B_1, \ldots, B_n\}$ where:*

- $\forall_{i \in \{1,\ldots,n\}} B_i \subseteq \mathcal{B}_\Phi \wedge vol(B_i) > 0 \wedge B_i \subseteq \mathcal{S}_\Phi$
- $\forall_{i,j \in \{1,\ldots,n\} \wedge i \neq j}\ vol(B_i \cap B_j) = 0$
- $\bigcup_{i=1}^{n} B_i \subseteq \mathcal{S}_\Phi$

The solution space $\mathcal{S}_\Phi$ of the path condition Φ is approximated with a joint cover of $\mathcal{S}_\Phi^\boxplus = <\mathcal{S}_\Phi^\square, \mathcal{S}_\Phi^\blacksquare>$ of the outer and inner cover box where $\mathcal{S}_\Phi^\blacksquare \subseteq \mathcal{S}_\Phi^\square$.

Constraints over Integer Domains and Mixed Domains: The presented approach works also for integer domains and mixed integer constrains (i.e., constraints which contain both integer and floating variables). As suggested in [10], we can handle integer variables as floating variables when each domain modification is followed by rounding the computed bounds to the nearest integer inside the interval domain. The resulting integer value is represented as a point interval to be conform to the definitions above of the solution space enclosure.

Disjunctive Domains: Consider the case when a variable x is defined over the union of intervals $[-100, 2] \cup [7, 100] \cup [200, 500]$. We can define the variable x over the interval $[-100, 500]$ and add the constraint

$$min(x - 2, min(max(7 - x, x - 100), 500 - x)) \leq 0$$

Note that such operations are not differentiable. However, constraint reasoning techniques need only that the operations can be evaluated over the intervals.

4.6.2. Solution Space of Constraints Over Data Structures

The computation of the solution space for constraints over data structures deserves special interest. Such constraints are called heap constraints. The solution space in the case of data structure variables is discrete. Quantifying the solution space means counting the model formed by the constraints. As before, we restrict ourselves to finite input domains. Consequently, the number of possible heap nodes in the input domain is finite.

We propose to use Korat [12] to count the input data structure that satisfy a constraint over data structures within pre-defined bounds. Korat is a framework for the constraint-based generation of structurally complex inputs for Java programs. Korat provides also efficient counting of input data structures. Korat generates the inputs by solving constraints written as a boolean method called *repOk*. The body of such a method can contain any arbitrary complex predicate. The scope of the input domain is specified using specific Korat methods. Scope methods are used to specify bounds on the size of the input data structures and bounds on the definition domain of the primitive fields of the data structure.

We encode the constraints we obtain from symbolic execution as a predicate in the *repOk* methods. Korat counts then the data structures that satisfy the constraints for a given scope.

Example: Consider the Java code in Listing 4.1 for swapping a node in a linked list. The field `element` represent the integer value of the node. The field `next` represent the next node in the list. The method `swapNode` updates the input list which is referenced by the parameter `this`. The update is done through a nonlinear condition on the nodes `n` and `next`.

```
class Node {
 int element;
 Node next;

 Node swapNode () {
   if(next!=null) {
     if(element > next.element) {
      //location to analyze
      Node n = next;
      next = n.next;
      n.next = this;
      return n;
     }
   }
   return this;
 }
}
```

Listing 4.1: Example swapping a node in a linked list

We illustrate now the use of Korat to count the data structure models. First of all we scope our domain, and assume that the nodes can take the values 1 or 2. Additionally, we bound the size of the linked list to 2 nodes. These bounds are passed to Korat via its scope methods.

The path condition to reach the second branching condition in the swapNode (i.e., the location at line 8) is:

```
node!=null ∧ node.next!= null ∧ node.next!=node ∧
node.element>node.next.element
```

We pass the path condition to the repOk method of Korat. The total number of of valid input data structures that satisfy the path condition under the specified scope is 17. This means, there is 17 possible inputs to reach the location at line 8 of the code in Listing 4.1.

Remark: Constraints over numerical domains that contain transitive dependencies on the data structure encoded by the heap constraints are also counted by Korat.

4.7. Probability of Satisfying a Path Condition

The theory of probability is a classical model to deal with uncertainty. A probabilistic model is defined by a set of random variables and a set of events. A random variable is a function from the sample space to the real numbers. An event is an assignment of values to all the variables of the model.

We want to compute the probability of satisfying a path condition. In our case here, the model is the path condition and the random variables are the variables of the path condition. An event is an assignment of values to the variables such that the path condition is satisfied.

In order to specify a probabilistic model, a full joint probability distribution should be explicitly or implicitly used. This distribution assigns a probability measure to each possible event. Such distributions can be provided by an operational profile.

Operational profile Example: Consider a method with a single input variable x defined over a floating domain. A possible operational profile can be of the form $OP = \{(x \in [1, 10], 0.3), (x \in [20, 30], 0.7)\}$. This means that the probability that the variable x takes values from the interval $[1, 10]$ is 0.3 and that it takes values from $[20, 30]$ is 0.7.

More formally, an OP can be defined as $OP = \{(\mathcal{C}_i, p_i) | i \in \{1, ..., L\}, \sum_{i=1}^{L} p_i = 1\}$: it is a set of pairs $(\mathcal{C}_i, p_i)$ where $\mathcal{C}_i$ represents constraints over the definition domain to describe a possible operational scenario, and p_i is the probability that an operational input belongs to $\mathcal{C}_i$.

4.7.1. Probability of a Path Condition over Data Structures

For heap path conditions, we use model counting as described in Section 4.6.2. Let $\#(c_i)$ denotes the function which counts the number of elements from a definition domain $\mathcal{D}$, which satisfy c_i. The probability of c_i is then: $\mathbb{P}(c_i) = \#(c_i)/\#\mathcal{D}$.

Consider we have the following operational profile:

$$OP = \{(\mathcal{C}_i, p_i) | i \in \{1, ..., L\}, \sum_{i=1}^{L} p_i = 1\}$$

For a path condition Φ, it follows from the law of total probability:

$$\mathbb{P}(\Phi | OP) = \sum_{i=1}^{L} \mathbb{P}(\Phi | \mathcal{C}_i).p_i$$

Furthermore, it follows from the definition of conditional probability:

$$\mathbb{P}(\Phi | \mathcal{C}_i) = \frac{\mathbb{P}(\Phi \wedge \mathcal{C}_i)}{\mathbb{P}(\mathcal{C}_i)}$$

Consequently, we obtain:

$$\mathbb{P}(\Phi | OP) = \sum_{i=1}^{L} \frac{\#(\Phi \wedge \mathcal{C}_i)}{\#(\mathcal{C}_i)}.p_i$$

4.7.2. Probability of a Path Condition over Numeric Domains

Definition 4.11. *(Probability of a Path Condition) The probability of a path condition* $\Phi = <\mathcal{V}_\Phi, \mathcal{B}_\Phi, \mathcal{C}_\Phi>$ *given the indicator function* $\mathbb{1}_{\mathcal{S}_\Phi}(x) : \mathbb{R}^{|\mathcal{V}_\Phi|} \rightarrow \{1, 0\}$ *defined as follows:*

$$\mathbb{1}_{\mathcal{S}_\Phi}(\mathbf{x}) = \begin{cases} 1, & if\, \mathbf{x} \in \mathcal{S}_\Phi \\ 0, & if\, \mathbf{x} \notin \mathcal{S}_\Phi \end{cases}$$

is defined as:

$$\mathbb{P}(\Phi) = \int_{\mathcal{B}_\Phi} \mathbb{1}_{\mathcal{S}_\Phi}(\mathbf{x}).f_{\mathcal{V}_\Phi}(\mathbf{x})d\mathbf{x}$$

where $f_{\mathcal{V}_\Phi}$ *is a full joint probability density function (p.d.f) over the path constraint variables* $\mathcal{V}_\Phi$*,* $\mathcal{S}_\Phi$ *the solution space of the path condition and* $\mathcal{B}_\Phi$ *the definition domain of the path condition.*

Generally, the multidimensional integral in Def. 4.11 may have no closed form solution since the constraints of a path condition may define a complex nonlinear integration boundary. Our approach approximates the solution space of a path condition with a joint cover $\mathcal{S}_\Phi^{\boxplus} = <\mathcal{S}_\Phi^{\square}, \mathcal{S}_\Phi^{\blacksquare}>$.

Monte Carlo methods provide an approach to approximate the value of multidimensional integrals by randomly sampling N points in the multidimensional definition space and averaging the integral values at the samples.

Definition 4.12. *(Monte Carlo Integration) Let* $\mathcal{S}_\Phi \subseteq \mathbb{R}^{|\mathcal{V}_\Phi|}$*, and* B *a* $|\mathcal{V}_\Phi|$*-dimensional box. If we sample uniformly* N *random values* $\{x_1, \ldots, x_n\}$ *inside* B*, then by the law of large numbers it follows:*

$$\int_B \mathbb{1}_{\mathcal{S}_\Phi}(\mathbf{x}).f_{\mathcal{V}_\Phi}(x)dx \approxeq \widehat{I}_{\mathcal{S}_\Phi}(B, f_{\mathcal{V}_\Phi}) = \frac{\sum_{i=1}^{N} \mathbb{1}_{\mathcal{S}_\Phi}(x_i).f_{\mathcal{V}_\Phi}(x_i)}{N}.vol(B)$$

where $vol(B)$ *the volume of the box* B*.*

By the central limit theorem, one can estimate the uncertainty in the approximation of the Monte Carlo integration.

Definition 4.13. *(Standard Deviation of the Estimate) The standard deviation of the approximation of the integral* $\widehat{I}_{\mathcal{S}_\Phi}(B, f_{\mathcal{V}_\Phi})$ *follows from the central limit theorem as follows:*

$$\sigma(\widehat{I}_{\mathcal{S}_\Phi}(B, f_{\mathcal{V}_\Phi})) = \frac{vol(B)}{N}\sqrt{\sum_{i=1}^{N}(\mathbb{1}_{\mathcal{S}_\Phi}(x_i).f_{\mathcal{V}_\Phi}(x_i))^2 - \frac{(\sum_{i=1}^{N}(\mathbb{1}_{\mathcal{S}_\Phi}(x_i).f_{\mathcal{V}_\Phi}(x_i))^2}{N}}$$

The standard deviation describes a statistical estimate of the error on the integral approximation.

Definition 4.14. *(Approximate Probability of a Path Condition) Given a joint box cover* $\mathcal{S}_\Phi^{\boxplus} = <\mathcal{S}_\Phi^{\square}, \mathcal{S}_\Phi^{\blacksquare}>$ *of the solution space of a path condition* Φ*, an approximation for the probability of satisfying* Φ *is:*

$$[\mathbb{P}(\Phi)] = \sum_{B_i \in \mathcal{S}_\Phi^{\square}} \left[\frac{\sum_{i=1}^{N} \mathbb{1}_{\mathcal{S}_\Phi}(x_i).f_{\mathcal{V}_\Phi}(x_i)}{N}.vol(B_i)\right]$$

Monte Carlo Integration may suffer from a slow convergence rate especially when the approximated integral gets close to zero. One may need a large number of random samples N to approximate the probability to some given confidence. Stratified sampling and importance sampling are well-know techniques to reduce the variance of Monte Carlo integration methods. We integrate these techniques in our approximation as follows:

Definition 4.15. *(Approximate Probability of a Path Condition) Given a joint box cover* $\mathcal{S}_\Phi^{\boxplus} = <\mathcal{S}_\Phi^{\square}, \mathcal{S}_\Phi^{\blacksquare}>$ *of the solution space of a path condition* Φ*, an approximation for the probability of satisfying* Φ *is:*

$$[\mathbb{P}(\Phi)] = \sum_{B_i \in \mathcal{S}_\Phi^{\square}} \left[\frac{\sum_{i=1}^{N} \mathbb{1}_{\mathcal{S}_\Phi}(x_i).f_{\mathcal{V}_\Phi}(x_i)}{N}.\mathbb{P}(B_i)\right] = \sum_{B_i \in \mathcal{S}_\Phi^{\square}} \left[\widehat{p}_i.\mathbb{P}(B_i)\right]$$

The scheme $\sum_{B_i \in \mathcal{S}_\Phi^{\square}} \left[\widehat{p}_i.\mathbb{P}(B_i)\right]$ integrates both stratified sampling and importance sampling. Each box B_i can be written as the Cartesian product of intervals: $B_i : [a_1, b_1] \times [a_2, b_2] \times \ldots \times [a_i, b_i]$. $\mathbb{P}(B_i)$ is defined then as: $\mathbb{P}(B_i) = \mathbb{P}_{x_1}([a_1, b_1]).\mathbb{P}_{x_2}([a_2, b_2]) \ldots \mathbb{P}_{x_i}([a_i, b_i])$ with $\mathbb{P}_{x_i}([a_i, b_i]) = \int_{a_i}^{b_i} f_i(x_i)dx_i$ and f_i the probability distribution function over the variable x_i. Such a distribution can be specified in an OP.

4.8. Looping Constructs: Incremental Probabilistic Symbolic Execution

Usually a bound on the exploration depth is set when executing a program symbolically. Instead of setting a static bound, we introduce a probabilistic bound P_{depth}. Given an OP, the user may be interested in only exploring program paths which have a probability higher than P_{depth}. Algorithm 10 sketches our extension to symbolic execution to incrementally compute the path condition probabilities. For a given program starting with statement s, an initial update $\mathcal{U}_0$, an operational profile OP, and a probabilistic bound P_{depth} the call of *IncProbSymExe*($\mathcal{U}_0$, s, *true*, $\emptyset$, OP, P_{depth}) will return the path conditions of all feasible paths of the program together with their computed probabilities. Until a branching condition is found the procedure accumulates the state changes in form of update expressions (lines 5-7). In the case of a branching statement a new path condition is constructed for each branch outcome based of the current path condition Φ and the branch conditions ($cond(s)$ and $\neg cond(s)$). Only if a constructed path condition is satisfiable, algorithm 11 computes its probability (usually SAT solving is less expensive than model counting). The corresponding branch code is further proceeded if the computed probability is higher than the bound P_{depth}. Algorithm 11 splits the conjunction (line 1) as defined in Def. 4.5. It then computes the probability of Φ as described in Section 4.7.

4.9. Adaptive Constrained White-Box Statistical Testing

Algorithm 12 works until line 11 as explained in Section 3.10. If the stopping criteria (line 6) is not reached, then algorithm 12 executes the black-box test cases and computes the posterior failure rate (line 9). Then faults are repaired.

Algorithm 10: An abstract incremental probabilistic symbolic execution procedure – IncProbSymExe

```
Data: 𝒰 : Update, s : Statement, Φ : Formula, PCs : Set<Formula>
      OP = {(D_i, p_i) | i ∈ {1, ..., L}, Σ_{i=1}^{L} p_i = 1}, P_depth
1  begin
2      if s = ∅ then
3          PCs ← PCs ∪ Φ
4      else
5          while ¬branch(s) do
6              𝒰 ← 𝒰 ∘ update(s)
7              s ← next(s)
8          if SAT(Φ ∧ {𝒰}cond(s)) then
9              ℙ(Φ ∧ {𝒰}cond(s)) ← computeProbs(OP, Φ, {𝒰}cond(s))
10             if ℙ(Φ ∧ {𝒰}cond(s)) ≥ P_depth then
11                 IncProbSymExe(𝒰, first(s), Φ ∧ {𝒰}cond(s), PCs)
12         if SAT(Φ ∧ {𝒰}¬cond(s)) then
13             ℙ(Φ ∧ {𝒰}¬cond(s)) ← computeProbs(OP, Φ, {𝒰}¬cond(s))
14             if ℙ(Φ ∧ {𝒰}¬cond(s)) ≥ P_depth then
15                 IncProbSymExe(𝒰, first(s), Φ ∧ {𝒰}¬cond(s), PCs)
16         return <PCs, Probabilities>
```

P_{depth} is computed as $\frac{1}{|\mathcal{T}_{OP}|}$, where $|\mathcal{T}_{OP}|$ is the total number of test cases that must be executed from the operational profile (OP). This describes the smallest probability that a test case can take to be conform to the probability distribution of the operational profile.

Using the computed P_{depth} the incremental symbolic execution is called (line 12) to extract a set of path conditions together with their probability of satisfaction according to the OP, $PC_i, \mathbb{P}(PC_i)$. Then, algorithm 12 is recursively called using the new extracted operational profile $PC_i, \mathbb{P}(PC_i)$ line (13).

Algorithm 11: Compute formula probability and search depth – computeProbs

Data: $OP = \{(D_i, p_i) | i \in \{1, ..., L\}, \ \sum_{i=1}^{L} p_i = 1\}$,
$\Phi : Formula, c : Formula$

begin
  $<\Phi_{dep}, \Phi_{notdep}> = split(\Phi, c)$
  $\mathbb{P}(\Phi) \leftarrow \mathbb{P}(\Phi(notdep))$ //Previously computed and in cache
  $\mathbb{P}(\Phi) \leftarrow \mathbb{P}(\Phi) + \mathbb{P}(\Phi_{dep} | OP)$
  return $\mathbb{P}(\Phi)$

4.10. Discussion

In algorithm 12, the incremental symbolic execution is restarted at each iteration of the algorithm (line 12). This is explained by the fact that after fault repair, the behavior of the software program is expected to change. Therefore, it may happen that some path condition disappear after fault repair. Consequently, it is necessary to restart symbolic execution at each iteration of the algorithm.

Furthermore, we do use the predictive approach presented in Section 3.11, since the available test inputs per path condition may be not sufficient to train the Gaussian process.

Algorithm 12: Adaptive Constrained White-Box Statistical Testing - adaptiveWhiteBox

Require: $OP = \{(\mathcal{D}_i, p_i) | i \in \{1, ..., L\}, \sum_{i=1}^{L} p_i = 1\}$
Δ : maximal allowed test time
$1 - \alpha$: confidence level
d : margin of error
//1. Initialization
$\mathcal{T}_{OP}$ = computeIntialTestCases(OP)
$\{(\mathcal{D}_i, p_i, \hat{\mu_i}, {\sigma_i}^2, {\beta_1}^i, {\beta_2}^i) | i \in \{1, \ldots, L\}\}$ = computePriorFailure($\mathcal{T}_{OP}$)
Repair faults if failures are revealed
//2. Adaptive constrained test selection
while true **do**
($\mathcal{T}_{OP}$, opt) = computeOptimalTestCases($\{(\mathcal{D}_i, p_i, \hat{\mu_i}, {\sigma_i}^2, {\beta_1}^i, {\beta_2}^i) | i \in \{1, \ldots, L\}\}$)
if Δ passed or (opt = $L \wedge \mathcal{SC}(\mathcal{T}_{OP}) = 100\%$) **then**
break;
end if
$\{(\mathcal{D}_i, p_i, \hat{\mu_i}, {\sigma_i}^2, {\beta_1}^i, {\beta_2}^i) | i \in \{1, \ldots, L\}\}$ = computePosteriorFailureRate($\mathcal{T}_{OP}$, $\{(\mathcal{D}_i, p_i, \hat{\mu_i}, {\sigma_i}^2, {\beta_1}^i, {\beta_2}^i) | i \in \{1, \ldots, L\}\}$)
Repair faults
$P_{depth} \leftarrow \frac{1}{|\mathcal{T}_{OP}|}$
$(PC_i, \mathbb{P}(PC_i)) \leftarrow$ *IncProbSymExe*($\mathcal{U}_0$, *s*, *true*, $\emptyset$, *OP*, P_{depth})
$adaptiveWhiteBox(PC_i, \mathbb{PC}_{\sqsupset})$
opt = 1
end while
return $\widehat{R} = \sum_{i=1}^{L} p_i.(1 - \hat{\mu_i})$, $\text{var}[\widehat{R}] = \sum_{i=1}^{L} {p_i}^2 \frac{{\sigma_i}^2}{|\mathcal{T}_{(\mathcal{D}_i, p_i)}|}$

5. Verification-Based Reliability Assessment

In the following we consider a white-box software component, where its provides and required methods are formally specified (e.g., JML contracts). Furthermore, we require a specification of its execution environment (e.g., provided by using the Palladio Component Model). We use in the following the KeY theorem prover as the deductive source code verification system to illustrate our approach. However, we believe that our approach can be easily extended to other deductive verification systems.

5.1. Problem Definition

Deductive source verification can automatically prove the correctness of a software with respect to a formal verification. If we formally verify the software program as well as its environment, then the verification system would certify the 100% reliability of the software system with total confidence (i.e., perfect reliability). However, usually it is not practical to verify the software program as well the execution environment. In such as case only the software program may be verified. In order to consider the execution environment of the software program, exhaustive testing is executed (verification-based testing). However, exhaustive testing is usually impractical for real work software systems. Furthermore, without doing exhaustive testing, we cannot make any statement about the reliability of the software under study. Existing reliability assessment approaches do not make use of the certainty gained after the verification of the software program and rely on verification for the generation of exhaustive test cases. Can we make use of the certainty gained from verification for the reliability assessment to avoid exhaustive testing?

Now, let us assume that verification is only done for the software program. Because of the semi-decidability of first-order logic, the KeY theorem prover may never terminate (e.g., because of existing software faults). If a timeout is set, then KeY would not close all proof obligations, i.e, some proof obligations will remain open. In such as case, the open branches are usually exhaustively tested to detect possible faults. However, in order to estimate the reliability of the software system, the whole software should be exhaustively tested as explained above.

We believe, however, that the closed proof obligations give us some certainty about the reliability of the software systems, and the open branches should reduce our confidence on the software reliability

5.2. Research Goals

Our first goal is to make it possible to assess the reliability of a software system without explicitly modeling the execution environment in the verification logic. This would allow us to quantify the reliability of the software system after verification is done without the need to exhaustively test it to take the environment into consideration.

The second goal, uses the first goal to quantify the reliability of the software system when some proof obligations are open. This means, our goal is to quantify the uncertainty produced by the open proof obligations on the reliability estimate.

5.3. Assumptions

The verification-based reliability assessment approach we present in this Chapter makes use of both the white-box and the black-box approaches from Chapters 4 and 3. Consequently, we adopt the same assumptions as in Section 4.3 and 3.4.

Furthermore, we assume that:

- a specification of the reliability of the execution environment is provided as described in Section 2.2.4.
- each required method is formally specified in order to be able to run the verification.

5.4. Motivating Example

Figure 5.1 shows a motivating example for our verification-based reliability assessment approach. The example shows a Palladio Component Model instance. The example consists of three software components. The `delegatedSort` component requires an `advancedSort` component and a `localSort` component. The dependencies between the components is described by the component service behavior model.

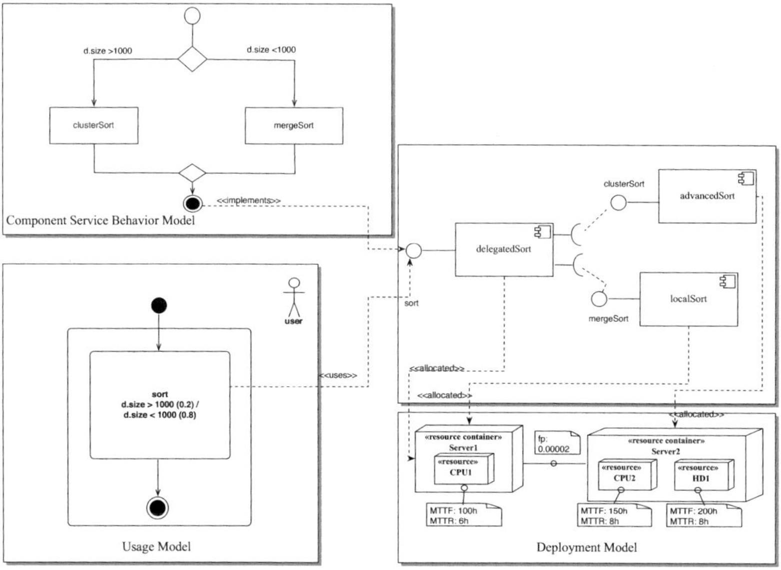

Figure 5.1.: Motivating Example – PCM Instance

```
/*@ ensures isSorted(\result); *@/
public Data delegatedSort(Data d){
  if(d.size < N){
   return mergeSort(d);
  }else{
   return clusterSort(d);
} }

/*@ ensures ...; *@/
public boolean isSorted(Data d);


/*@ ensures isSorted(\result); *@/
public Data mergeSort(Data d);


/*@ ensures isSorted(\result); *@/
public Data clusterSort(Data d);
```

Figure 5.2.: Motivating example Code

The provided method `sort` is supposed to sort the data of a class `Data` which is provided as argument `d`. If the size of the data is smaller than some number `1000`, then the method `mergeSort` provided by the component `localSort` is invoked to perform the sorting, otherwise the method `clusterSort` provided by the component `advancedSort` is invoked.

The usage model specifies how the provided method `sort` will be called by the user. According to the usage model, we expect that `d.size > 1000` in 20% of the cases, and `d.size < 1000` in 80%. The Palladio Component Model uses the usage model and the component service behavior model to solve parameter dependencies, and output an operational profile for each provided method.

Assume now that the component `advancedSort` is a COTS component and its code is not available. We use then our black-box reliability assessment approach to estimate the reliability of its provided method `clusterSort`.

Assume that the component `localSort` is not planned for formal verification, but its source code is at hand. We use then our white-box reliability approach to estimate the reliability of the provided method `mergeSort`.

Using KeY the correctness of the implementation in Figure 5.2 of `delegatedSort` wrt. its specification can be easily proved—but, how reliable is the method in practice?

The deployment model as depicted in Figure 5.1, defines the execution environment consisting of physical computing nodes connected via network links. Each component is deployed on a physical computing node. The availability of each physical node can be computed as described in Section 2.2.4. Furthermore, the method `clusterSort` is called via network and the failure probability of the network should be considered when estimating the reliability.

5.5. Reliability Assessment When Proof Attempt Succeeds

Assume, that we used KeY to verify the correctness of the provided method `sort` of the component `delegatedSort` and the proof attempt succeeded. In such a case we obtain a set of closed proof obligations with PCs, $PC^c = \{PC^c_1, PC^c_2, \ldots, PC^c_m\}$.

The reliability of the software is thus estimated as:

$$\hat{R} = \sum_{i=1}^{m} \mathbb{P}(PC^c_i|OP).(1 - FR_i)$$

where $\mathbb{P}(PC^c_i|OP)$ the probability of executing the path condition PC^c_i given the operational profile OP, computed as explained in Chapter 4. Let M be the set of required methods called within PC^c_i, that is $M = \{m^1_{required}, \ldots, m^{|M|}_{required}\}$. Then, FR_i is defined as follows:

$$FR_i = (1 - Av(e_i)).\prod_{j=1}^{|M|} \hat{\mu}(m^j_{required}).r^j_{cr}$$

$$FR_i = 1 - Av(e_i).\prod_{j=1}^{|M|}(1 - \hat{\mu}(m^j_{required})).r^j_{cr}$$

with $Av(e_i)$ the availability of the execution environment where the program path represented by PC^c_i is executed (i.e, the availability of the physical computing node where the component `delegatedSort` is deployed), and $\hat{\mu}(m^j_{required})$ is the failure rate of the method $m^j_{required}$, and r^j_{cr} is the reliability of call and return of the required method $m^j_{required}$ defined as:

- $r^j_{cr} = 1$, if $m^j_{required}$ is called within the same physical computing node as the program path represented by PC^c_i.
- $r^j_{cr} = (1 - fp(L))^2$, otherwise, where $fp(L)$ is the failure probability of the network link used for the two message transports call and return.

A software component per definition should encapsulate its state or behavior behind an interface. Furthermore, a component is only dependent on its framework and other components in its operating environment, where the dependencies are explicitly defined through the required and provided interfaces.

Therefore, we can assume that the failure rate of the required methods $M = \{m^1_{required}, \ldots, m^{|M|}_{required}\}$ called within PC^c_i are independent.

The failure rate of $m^j_{required}$ can be estimated using:

- the black-box reliability assessment approach presented in Chapter 3, if the component implementing $m^j_{required}$ is black-box
- the white-box reliability assessment approach presented in Chapter 4, if the component implementing $m^j_{required}$ is white-box
- the approach presented in this Section, if $m^j_{required}$ is implemented by a component we want to formally verify its correctness

In all cases, a failure rate $\hat{\mu}_{m^j_{required}}$ and a variance $\hat{\sigma}^2_{m^j_{required}}$ are estimated for each $m^j_{required}$.

Recall that for independent random variables $X_1, \ldots, X_n$, we have:

$$
\begin{aligned}
var(\prod_{i=1}^{n} X_i) &= E[(\prod_{i=1}^{n} X_i)^2] - (E[\prod_{i=1}^{n} X_i])^2 \\
&= E[(\prod_{i=1}^{n} X_i^{\,2})] - (\prod_{i=1}^{n} E[X_i])^2 \\
&= \prod_{i=1}^{n} E[X_i^{\,2}] - \prod_{i=1}^{n} (E[X_i])^2 \\
&= \prod_{i=1}^{n} (var(X_i) + (E[X_i])^2) - \prod_{i=1}^{n} (E[X_i])^2
\end{aligned}
$$

Consequently, the variance the failure rate for PC_i^c can be computed as follows:

$$
\hat{\sigma}_i^2 = \prod_{i=1}^{|M|} (\hat{\sigma}^2_{m^j_{required}} + (\hat{\mu}_{m^j_{required}})^2) - \prod_{i=1}^{n} (\hat{\mu}_{m^j_{required}})^2
$$

Now using equation (3.5b), the variance of the reliability estimate $\hat{R}$ can be computed as follows:

$$
\begin{aligned}
var(\hat{R}) &= \sum_{i=1}^{m} \mathbb{P}(PC_i^c|OP)^2 \frac{\hat{\sigma}_i^2}{n_i} \\
&= \sum_{i=1}^{m} \mathbb{P}(PC_i^c|OP)^2 \frac{\hat{\sigma}_i^2}{\#(OP)\mathbb{P}(PC_i^c|OP)} \\
&= \sum_{i=1}^{m} \mathbb{P}(PC_i^c|OP) \frac{\hat{\sigma}_i^2}{\#(OP)}
\end{aligned}
$$

where n_i the number of test cases (samples) executed from PC_i^c, defined as $n_i = \#(OP)\mathbb{P}(PC_i^c|OP)$, with $\#(OP)$ the cardinality of the input domain which we assume finite. Since PC_i^c is verified as correct, this means that all possible inputs satisfying PC_i^c will execute it correctly. Since the variance $\hat{\sigma}_i^2$ is computed based on the fact that PC_i^c is verified as correct, then it follows that n_i is the number of all test cases that can execute PC_i^c.

Now, if a confidence level $1 - \alpha$ is required for the reliability estimate $\hat{R}$ with a margin of error d, then we can compute based on the variance $var(\hat{R})$, the actual margin of error as:

$$z_{\frac{\alpha}{2}} \frac{\sqrt{var(\hat{R})}}{\sqrt{\#(OP}}$$

where $z_{\frac{\alpha}{2}}$ is the upper $\frac{\alpha}{2}$ critical value for the standard normal distribution.

If $d < z_{\frac{\alpha}{2}} \frac{\sqrt{var(\hat{R})}}{\sqrt{\#(OP}}$, then testing is required. In such a case, since all PCs are correct, then the black-box reliability assessment approach presented in Section 3.10, can be used to decrease $var(\hat{R})$ and hence decrease the margin of error d.

5.6. Reliability Assessment When Proof Attempt not Succeed

If the proof attempt does not succeed, then we obtain open proof obligations with PCs, $PC^o = \{PC_1^o, PC_2^c, \ldots, PC_p^o\}$. Here we differentiate between two cases: (i) some proof obligations are closed, (ii) all proof obligations are open.

5.6.1. Some Proof Obligations are Closed

In such as case we can estimate the reliability as well as its variance as shown in Section 5.5.

The PC^os decrease our confidence on the reliability estimate to

$$c = 1 - \sum_{i=1}^{p} \mathbb{P}(PC_i^o | OP)$$

If the confidence c or the reliability estimate $\hat{R}$ are less than the user required values, then we execute statistical testing only on the PC^os. The PCs identified by KeY define disjoint input sets of the software program. Consequently, symbolic execution defines a fine grained representation of the OP:

$$OP^{sym} = \{(PC_i, \mathbb{P}(PC_i|OP))|i = 1, 2, \ldots, (n+p), \sum_{i=1}^{n+p} \mathbb{P}(PC_i|OP)) = 1\}$$

that we use as input to our adaptive test selection approach. The approach uses the symbolically estimated reliability and the fine grained OP^{sym} to efficiently select test cases across the PCs. Assume that the adaptive selection approach requires that n_c test cases should be selected from the PC^cs and n_o from the PC^os. We do not execute PC^cs, but we take their failure rates, the variances of the failure rate as well as the probabilities of PC^c to be executed into account when computing the required number of test cases to estimate the unknown failure rate of the PC^os and bound its unknown variance. Therefore, instead of executing $n_o + n_c$ test cases, we execute only n_o test cases.

5.6.2. All Proof Obligations are Open

In such as case, the white-box reliability assessment approach is used to estimate the reliability and its variance.

5.7. Recursive Method Calls and Looping Constructs

In our approach we treat recursive method calls and looping constructs by bounded unrolling. This allows full automation of the approach. The standard solution is to set a static bound on the exploration depth. We guide the construction of the proof tree based on the user required reliability goal. Based on user reliability goal, our adaptive white-box approach (See Section 3) computes the required number n of test cases to be executed to reach the target reliability goal. Each test has a corresponding PC. Given an $OP = \{(\mathcal{D}_i, p_i) | i = 1, 2, \ldots, L, \sum_{i=1}^{L} p_i = 1\}$, each test execution from a subdomain $\mathcal{D}_i$ has at least the probability p_i/n. At each unrolling attempt of a loop we compute the probability of the obtained PC and unroll the loop if $\mathbb{P}(PC|\mathcal{D}_i) < p_i/n$. This bound is computed based on the reliability goals and adaptively updated after test cases are executed and reliability goals not reached (see previous section when proof attempt not succeeds).

6. Validation

In this Chapter, we experimentally evaluate the goal of our approach in reducing the number of test cases required to reach a target confidence on the reliability estimate. Our approach is composed of three techniques (i) Black-Box reliability assessment, (ii) White-Box reliability assessment, and (iii) Verification-based reliability assessment. Consequently, we experimentally evaluate the ability of each of the three techniques in reducing the testing overhead. A subset of the presented case studies have been presented in our publications [72] and [73]. Furthermore, we study the ability of our approach in reducing the sensitivity of the reliability estimation to variations of the operational profile.

6.1. Black-Box Reliability Assessment

The goals of the following experimental validation are:

1. validate the reliability estimation efficiency and accuracy of the black-box reliability assessment approach compared to state-of-the-art statistical testing approaches

2. validate the prediction accuracy of the non-parametric reliability prediction model compared to state-of-the-art reliability models

6.1.1. Reliability Estimation Efficiency and Accuracy

We conduct a set of experiments on two real subject programs to evaluate the performance of the adaptive constrained statistical test selection (ACSTS) approach against the standard proportional test selection approach as proposed by Musa [69] (PS), and the (theoretical [1]) optimal test selection approach (OS) with respect to the estimated reliability accuracy and precision.

6.1.1.1. Subject Programs

Two real subject programs are used to evaluate the efficiency of ACSTS:

TCAS: Traffic Alert and Collision Avoidance System prevents aircraft from midair collisions. The correct versions, 41 faulty versions of the programs as well as a suite of 1608 test cases were downloaded from [84]. TCAS is 173 LOCs big.

Space: a language oriented user interface developed by the European Space Agency. It allows the user to describe the configuration of an array of antennas with a high level language. The correct version as well as the 38 faulty versions and a test suite of 13, 585 test cases are downloaded from the software-artifact infrastructure repository (http://sir.unl.edu). In these experiments, three faulty versions are not used because we did not find test cases that failed on these faulty versions. Space is 9126 LOCs big.

A failure of an execution is determined by comparing the outputs of the faulty version and the correct version of the program. A failure is a deviation from the expected output. The failure rates for both studied programs are empirically computed by executing all the available test cases against each faulty version of a program and recording the number of failed test cases.

6.1.1.2. Operational Profiles

Operational profiles for TCAS and Space are not available. We create operational profiles for TCAS and Space as follows. We assume that in each sub-domain $\mathcal{D}_i$, all possible inputs are equally likely to arise. Hence, it follows that the number of sub-domains (greater or equal to two sub-domains) as well as the number of inputs in each sub-domain may not bias the statistical properties (i.e., variance and mean) of the estimated reliability. The estimated reliability is influenced by the probability of occurrence of the sub-domains, as well as the true failure rate of the tested software when executed with

[1] We assume here that we know the failure rates in advance, and we sample accordingly

inputs from each sub-domain. In that sense, we partition the test cases of TCAS and Space in six disjoint sub-domains. All six sub-domains contain the same number of test cases except for rounding issues. For each sub-domain, test cases are randomly selected without replacement from the pool of test cases. In order to minimize possible bias due to the choice of the test cases in each sub-domain, we repeat the allocation of the test cases of each subject program into the six sub-domains twice. This results into 2 possible allocations of the test cases to sub-domains $\mathcal{D}_i$ for each subject program.

We define two different profiles for the probability of occurrence of the sub-domains:

1. uniform profile: the probability of occurrence of each sub-domain is the same except for rounding error
2. optimal profile: the probability of occurrence of each sub-domain is proportional to the number of test cases allocated to each sub-domain using optimal allocation

These two profiles are some typical or extreme profiles and cannot represent all usage scenarios in field use.

Consequently, for each subject program, 4 different operational profiles are created.

The 1608 test cases of TCAS are partitioned into six disjoint classes each contains 268 test cases. The 13, 585 test cases of Space are partitioned into six disjoint classes: 2264, 2264, 2264, 2264, 2264 and 2265.

6.1.1.3. Performance Metrics

ACSTS, PS and OS are randomized test selection strategies. For statistical significance, we conduct 200 independent repetitions of each experiment for each test selection strategy.

We compare the performances of ACSTS, PS and OS by comparing the accuracy and precision of the estimated reliability by each approach. The accuracy of an estimate is a measure of how close the estimated value is to its true value. The precision of an estimate is a measure of how close the estimates measured from different samples are to another, when the samples are taken from the same data set. We use the sample variance as metric for the reliability estimation accuracy. The sample variance is an unbiased estimator of the variance. We use the *root mean squared error* (RMSE) to quantify the estimate precision.

Based on assumption 6 in Section 3.4, the reliability estimates delivered by ACSTS, PS, and OS are unbiased. Consequently, we can compare the relative efficiency of the estimates using the sample variance. For each experiment $\mathcal{E}$ we define the mean value of the reliability estimate ($\overline{R}$), its sample variance ($S^2_{199}(\widehat{R})$), its root mean squared error ($RMSE(\widehat{R})$), and the relative efficiency of the reliability estimator using ACSTS to PS and OS as follows:

$$\overline{R} = \frac{1}{200}\sum_{i=1}^{200}\widehat{R_i}, \quad S^2_{199}(\widehat{R}) = \frac{1}{199}\sum_{i=1}^{200}(\widehat{R_i} - \overline{R})^2$$

$$RMSE(\widehat{R}) = \sqrt{\frac{1}{200}\sum_{i=1}^{200}(\widehat{R_i} - R)^2}$$

$$\text{eff}(\widehat{R}_{ACSTS}, \widehat{R}_{PS}) = \frac{RMSE(\widehat{R}_{PS})}{RMSE(\widehat{R}_{ACSTS})}$$

$$\text{eff}(\widehat{R}_{ACSTS}, \widehat{R}_{OS}) = \frac{RMSE(\widehat{R}_{OS})}{RMSE(\widehat{R}_{ACSTS})}$$

where R is the true reliability calculated based on the true failure rates, $\widehat{R_i}$ the reliability estimate in repetition i of the experiment, $\widehat{R}_{ACSTS}$ the reliability estimate using ACSTS, $\widehat{R}_{PS}$ the reliability estimate using PS and $\widehat{R}_{OS}$ the reliability estimate using OS.

The differences in reliability mean values between the different test selection strategies is confirmed using the the non-parametric Matt-Whitney U test [97]. The differences between the sample variances are tested using the Brown-Forsythe test[97].

For each experiment and for each test selection strategy, we compute the reliability estimate at seven checkpoints: $200, 250, 350, \ldots, 500$. After 200 repetitions of the experiment, we compute the mean value, sample variance and the root mean square error of the reliability estimates for each test selection strategy. Note that the more test cases are executed the more will the variance of the estimator decrease. In addition, the experimental dataset is selected randomly from the population and the selection is repeated 200 times. Consequently, the selected dataset do not affect the efficiency and the generalizability of ACTS.

6.1.1.4. Experimental Results

The goal of this set of experiments is to assess the efficiency and precision of our reliability estimation approach.

Figures 6.2 and 6.1 present the sample means and sample variances for TCAS and Space respectively. The dashed lines are the true reliability values for the subject programs.

According to the experimental results, the means as well as the sample variances of the reliability estimates of ACSTS are closer to the true values than those of PS and OS. This is confirmed by the statistical tests Matt-Whitney U test and Brown-Forsythe test in tables 6.1 and 6.2. Both tables confirm that ACSTS significantly deliver more accurate reliability estimate that PS and OS.

		Variance		Mean	
Scenarios		ACSTS	OS	ACSTS	OS
TCAS profile1	PS	0/7	1/7	7/7	0/7
	OS	0/7	–	7/7	0/7
TCAS profile2	PS	0/7	0/7	7/7	0/7
	OS	0/7	–	7/7	–
TCAS profile3	PS	1/7	0/7	7/7	0/7
	OS	0/7	–	7/7	-
TCAS profile4	PS	0/7	0/7	7/7	0/7
	OS	0/7	–	7/7	–

Table 6.1.: Matt-Whitney U and Brown-Forsythe test results for the sample means and variances for TCAS

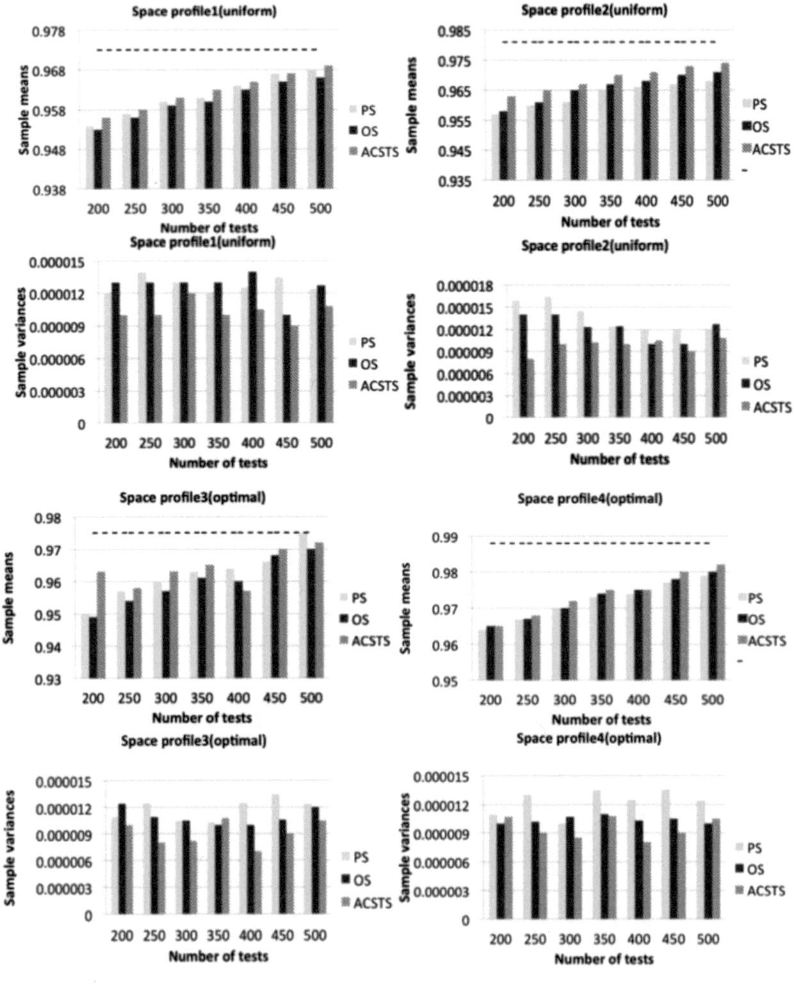

Figure 6.1.: Sample means and variances of the reliability estimates for Space

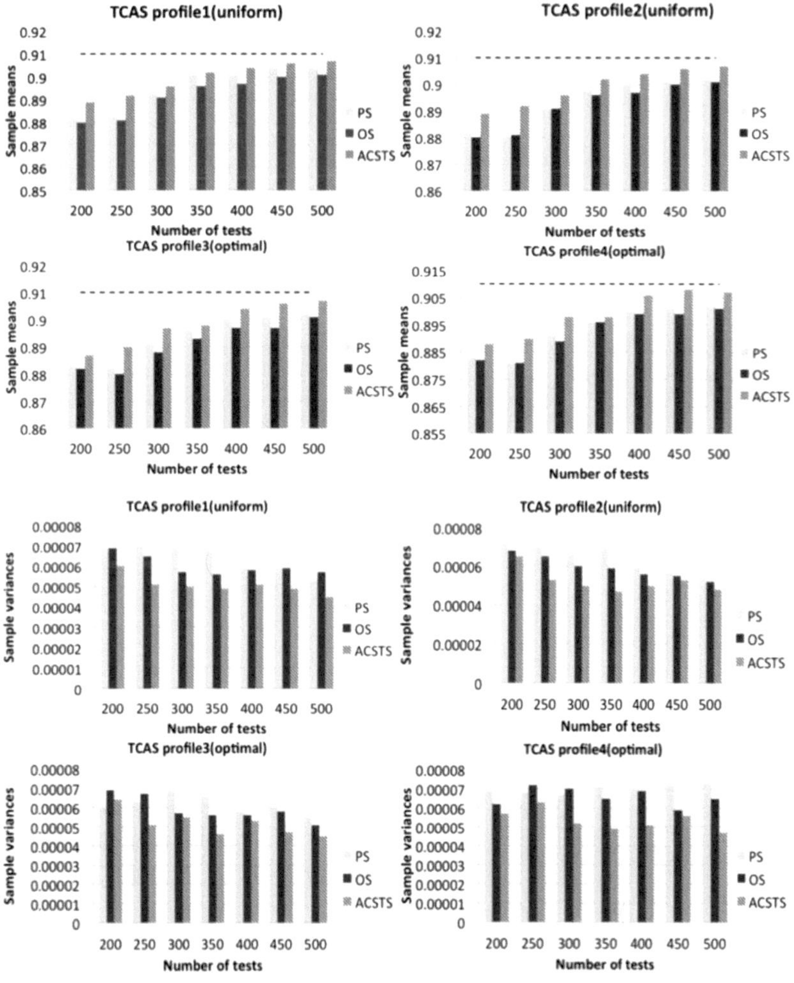

Figure 6.2.: Sample means and variances of the reliability estimates for TCAS

Scenarios		Variance		Mean	
		ACSTS	OS	ACSTS	OS
Space profile1	PS	0/7	4/7	6/7	0/7
	OS	0/7	–	7/7	–
Space profile2	PS	0/7	1/7	7/7	7/7
	OS	1/7	–	7/7	–
Space profile3	PS	1/7	1/7	7/7	5/7
	OS	1/7	–	5/7	–
Space profile4	PS	0/7	1/7	5/7	1/7
	OS	2/7	–	6/7	–

Table 6.2.: Matt-Whitney U and Brown-Forsythe test results for the sample means and variances for Space

During the experiments some failures are not observed, since the number of test cases used in each experiment is limited. Consequently a bias is introduced intro the reliability assessment. Figure 6.3 depicts the RMSEs for the studied approaches. Figure 6.3 shows that ACSTS provide low RMSEs compared to PS and OS. Consequently, ACSTS introduces less bias to the reliability estimate that PS and OS.

The computed mean of the relative efficiency of the reliability estimator using ACSTS compared to the one using PS for the TCAS experiments was $1,71$. This means, that PS will yield a reliability estimate as accurate as ACSTS only if 71 % more test cases are selected.

The computed mean of the relative efficiency of the reliability estimator using ACSTS compared to the one using OS for the TCAS experiments was $1,32$. This means, that OS will yield a reliability estimate as accurate as ACSTS only if 32 % more test cases are selected.

For the Space experiments, the relative efficiency to PS and OS estimators was $1,57$ and $1,23$ respectively.

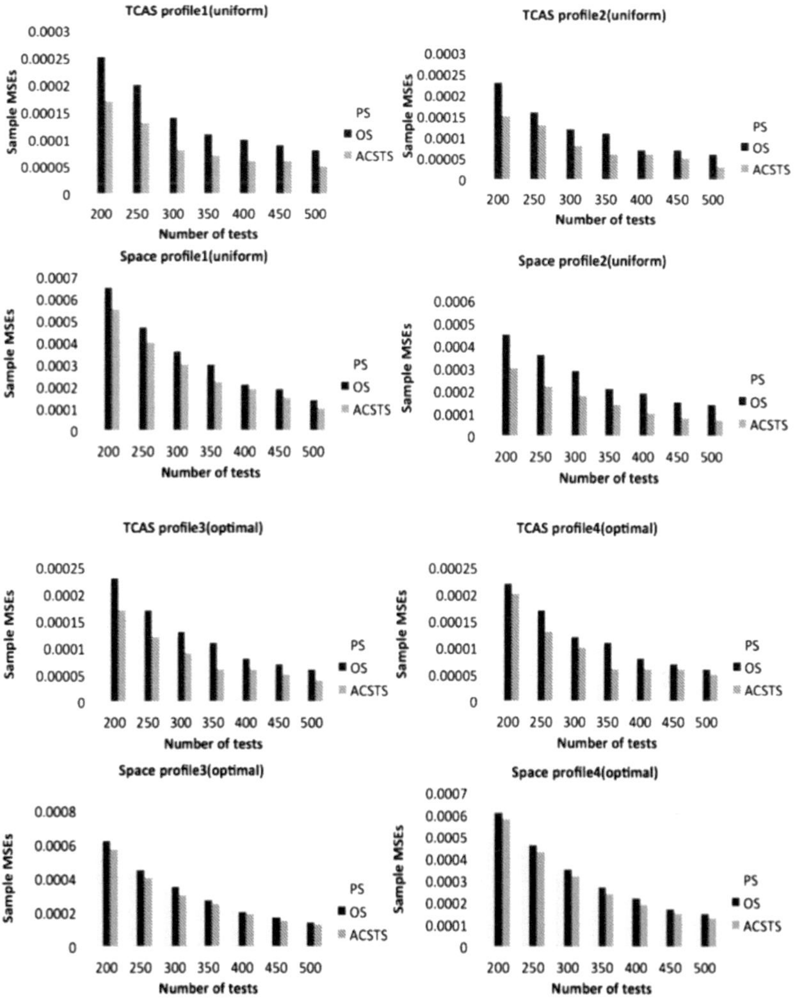

Figure 6.3.: RMSEs of the reliability estimates for TCAS and Space

6.1.1.5. Threats to Validity

There are several potential threats to the validity of the experiments, which are not limited to the following.

Construct validity: The experiments make use of operational profiles that were synthetically created based on available test suites. However, assumptions on the operational profiles may cause bias. In order to minimize possible bias due to the choices of the test cases in each sub-domain, the allocation of the test case to the sub-domains is repeated four times. We conduct then the experiments on all the created operational profiles.

Internal validity: The experiments compare the performance of test selection strategies with a focus on variance minimization. For each test selection strategy, 200 repetitions are conducted in each experiment to ensure confidence and statistical significance of the computed results. For each test selection strategy, the sample means, the sample variances and the RMSEs of the reliability estimates are compared using the Matt-Whitney U test and the Brown-Forsythe test to avoid possible statistical bias during the comparison. The used statistical tests are less sensitive to the data distribution allowing us to avoid assumptions about distribution of data. Another important threat to validity is that mutation and similar fault injection techniques were used to create faulty versions of the studied subject. Primary motivator for this is that faulty software version were not readily available. In addition, mutation-based fault injection have been actively used in software testing research like [3] and [32], where it has been shown that mutation is an effective approach to simulate realistic faults and provide a low-cost way to obtain sets used to obtain statistically significant conclusions. Consequently, while mutation techniques represent a potential threat to the validity of our experiments, we think it is a necessary technique to enlarge our data sets.

6.1.2. Prediction Accuracy of the Reliability Prediction Model

We perform an extensive evaluation of our reliability prediction model, described in Section 3.11, based on benchmark data set presented in [29]. The experiments are applied on bug and test data of the following open source software: Mylyn, Equinox framework and Eclipse JDT Core. Table 6.3, summarizes the experiments subjects.

System	Prediction Release	Time period	#Classes	#Versions	#Test Cases	#Post-rel. defects
Eclipse JDT Core	3.4	1.1.2005 – 6.17.2008	997	91	9, 135	463
Equinox framework	3.4	1.1.2005 – 6.25.2008	439	91	1, 616	279
Mylyn	3.4.1	1.17.2005 – 3.17.2009	2, 196	98	9, 189	677

Table 6.3.: Summary of characteristics of the considered benchmark systems

6.1.2.1. Experimental Setup and Metrics

For a given release of the subject software, we predict the post release failure rate for each class of the software. As independent variables for our Gauss regression-based reliability model, we use the number of existing test cases per class as well as two different software metrics as proposed by [29]:

1. Entropy of changes, which measures how changes to the source code are distributed in the software over a time interval when repairing faults. This metric computes the Shannon entropy of code changes [51]. The intuition of this metric is as follows: the more distributed the changes, the higher the complexity of the repair.

2. Entropy of source code, which extends the entropy of changes metric with the concept of the CK source code metric [21].

Both metrics have been computed and provided by [29].

We compare the prediction accuracy of our prediction model with:

1. the poisson generalized linear model (pGLM) [35], which is the basis of most of the software reliability models

2. the standard feed forward neural network, which has been used in [86], and outperformed the traditional software reliability models.

The prediction accuracy of the three prediction models is assessed using cross validation as follows: 80 % of the available classes are used for model training and the rest of classes are used to test the accuracy.

System	pGLM	Our Model	NN
Eclipse JDT Core	1.41(0.45)	1.03(0.36)	1.48(0.58)
Equinox framework	1.18(0.36)	1.03(0.26)	1.86(0.21)
Mylyn	1.23(0.08)	0.97(0.07)	1.31(0.33)

Table 6.4.: Entropy of Change Metric and # test cases

Since all models are randomized, we repeat our experiments 20 times. Each experiment gets different training set at each repetition. We report then the means of the estimated accuracy as well as the standard deviations. In order to compare the accuracy of the prediction models, we compute the root mean squared error (RMSE) between the actual and the predicted failure rate and the standard deviations over the 20 rauns of our experiments.

6.1.2.2. Evaluation Results Using Entropy of Change Metric

Table 6.4 summarizes the obtained performances of the evaluated prediction models when using entropy of changes and the number of test cases as independent for model training and prediction generation. As shown in table 6.4, our model yields better performance than both GLM and NN.

6.1.2.3. Evaluation Results Using Entropy of Source Code Metric

Table 6.5 summarizes the obtained performances of the evaluated prediction models when using entropy of source code and the number of test cases as independent for model training and prediction generation. As shown in table 6.5, our model yields better performance than both GLM, and better performance than NN with only one exception.

System	pGLM	Our Model	NN
Eclipse JDT Core	1.50(0.43)	0.96(0.23)	0.84(0.16)
Equinox framework	1.02(0.46)	0.92(0.21)	1.01(0.11)
Mylyn	1.26(0.32)	0.60(0.18)	1.25(0.37)

Table 6.5.: Entropy of Source Code Metric and # test cases

System	pGLM	Our Model	NN
Eclipse JDT Core	1.09(0.18)	1.03(0.40)	1.35(0.51)
Equinox framework	1.06(0.19)	0.92(0.24)	1.47(0.44)
Mylyn	1.13(0.39)	1.10(0.14)	1.35(0.23)

Table 6.6.: Only # test cases

6.1.2.4. Evaluation Results Without Software Metrics

Table 6.6 summarizes the obtained performances of the evaluated prediction models when using only the number of test cases as independent for model training and prediction generation. As shown in table 6.6, the performance of all models is poor compared to the case when software metric are used in tables 6.5 and 6.4.

Consequently, using software metrics for the prediction of the failure rate should increase the accuracy of our model.

6.2. White-box Reliability Assessment

The goals of the following validation are:

1. validate the accuracy and performance of our approach for computing the probability of path conditions compared to state-of-the-art approaches
2. show the applicability of our approach in aiding during program understanding and testing

3. validate the reliability estimate efficiency of the source code based reliability assessment approach compared to the black-box one

6.2.1. Implementation Details and Experimental Setup

Implementation: The prototype implementation of the probabilistic symbolic execution approach works with the symbolic execution engine of both KeY and Java Pathfinder. In order to split a path condition into disjoint sets of dependent constraints (see Def. 4.5), we model the constraints of each path condition as an undirected graph. The nodes of the graph are the constraints and the edges encode a dependency between the constraints: when constraints share the same input variable, an edge is added between the corresponding nodes. The computation of the connected components of the graph delivers us the split. In order to approximate the solution space of the constraints with a union of boxes, we base our implementation on an interval branch-and-prune constraint propagation framework, RealPaver [48]. The original RealPaver defines a user defined stopping criteria for the branch-and-prune algorithm by specifying (i) a maximal time budget per query, or (ii) the number of boxes reported per query, or (iii) lower bound on the size of box eligible for branching. We extended RealPaver by introducing a new stopping criteria which is more suitable to our probabilistic setting. Our goal when approximating the solution space of a path condition is the accurate computation of the probability of that path condition. The stopping criteria we introduced to the branch-and-prune algorithm imposes a used defined accuracy to the probability enclosure computed with Monte Carlo integration over the outer box cover. This allows us to control the branching part toward the boxes with the highest uncertainty in their computed probability. Consequently, we can efficiently reduce the uncertainty on the computed probability. In the case that the user required accuracy is too sharp and the required accuracy cannot be reached (because of the accumulation of rounding errors), the branch-and-prune algorithm stops when the lower bound on the size of the boxes reached (there are no more eligible boxes). All the following experiments are executed on an Mac Pro 2.66 Ghz with 8Gb of memory running OSX 10.9. Our tool implementation as well as the source code of the examples used in the experiments and the evaluation can be downloaded from [77].

Experimental Setup and Metrics: The following experiment evaluates how our approach compares with recently developed techniques, VolComp [91, 81] and qCoral [78, 11]. VolComp and qCoral are both recent techniques to approximate the probability of constraints. We use the built-in method NProbability (with the default parametrization) of the mathematical tool Mathematica [63] as a baseline for comparison. NProbability computes numerical integrals over predicates and probabilities, terminates when default accuracy requirements are met, and notifies when the accuracy requirements are not met.

VolComp bounds the solution with an interval. qCoral as well as our approach report the approximated solution and a standard deviation of the approximation. Our approach was configured as follows: (i) for the Monte Carlo integration, we use $N = 1000$ random samples, (ii) we set the lower bound on the size of the boxes eligible for branching to 10^{-5} and (iii) we set the required accuracy to 0.005 (the stopping criteria of our approach). We used the same configuration for qCoral, except the accuracy stopping criteria, since qCoral do not provide such a feature. Both our approach and qCoral implement randomized algorithms. We report averaged estimate and standard deviation over 20 runs.

To compare the three approaches, we selected benchmarks from the publicly available VolComp benchmarks [91]. The comparison subjects are: (i) ARTRIAL: the Framingham artial fibrillation risk calculator, (ii) CORONARY: the Framingham hypertension risk calculator, (iii) PACK: a model of a robot packing objects with varying weights and (vi) VOL: controller for filling a tank with fluid at certain rates. The path conditions for these programs are produced using VolComp.

6.2.1.1. Experimental Results

Table 6.7 summarizes the comparison between our approach and VolComp and qCoral. The first column of Table 6.7 state the program event whose probability is computed. The second column *#PCs* states the number of path conditions that reach the event.

In summary, our approach was almost always faster than qCoral, VolComp and NProbability (except for the VOL example, where VolComp was slightly faster). Note that the performance of `NProbability` depends usually on advanced settings. The tuning of such settings requires a deep understanding of the mathematical properties of the function to integrate. Such an understanding may not be derived from the code during the analysis. The efficiency of our approach compared to `qCoral` can be explained by the fact that we apply Monte Carlo Integration only on the outer box cover of the approximated solution space. However, `qCoral` samples randomly over the whole approximated solution space. Our approach required more than 30 minutes to compute the `Vol` event *count* ≥ 20. This is caused by the accumulation of rounding errors. Rounding errors accumulation magnifies when the quantified probability is close to 1. The rounding errors increase the uncertainty about the estimate. More uncertainty means more sampling.

We notice that the estimates computed by our approach as well as the estimates computed by `qCoral` fall within the bounds extracted by `VolComp`. The estimates delivered by our approach were closer to the exact solutions delivered by `NProbability` than the estimates produced by `qCoral` and `VolComp`. The precision of our approach is due to the integration of importance sampling and stratified sampling which reduce the uncertainty of the estimate. In addition, we control the branching step of the interval branch-and-prune algorithm toward branching the boxes with the highest uncertainty. This should decrease the overall uncertainty.

We observe that our approach as well as `qCoral` were equal slow for the benchmark `PACK`. The reason for that is that RealPaver generated only an outer box cover for the solution space. This means we sampled randomly over the whole solution space. This reduces the impact of our sampling strategy.

6.2.2. Applicability in Program Understanding and Testing

The goal of this evaluation is to see whether our approach can aid during program understanding and testing. We consider in our evaluation the Binary Tree implementation that was used by [90] to show that the Binary Tree example contains a bug in the `delete` method.

Event	#PCs	NProbability		VolComp		qCoral			our approach		
		solution	time(s)	bound	time(s)	avg. estimate	avg.σ	avg. time(s)	avg. estimate	avg.σ	avg. time(s)
ARTRIAL											
score ≥ 10	442	0.1343	476	[0.1343, 0.1343]	341	0.1343	0	183	0.1343	0	117
err ≤ 5	2260	0.9467	3879	[0.9387, 9573]	1390.24	0.9389	2.80e-04	685	0.9464	1.26e-04	344
CORONARY											
err ≥ 5	320	0.0006	3.44	[0, 0.0172]	23	0.00047	3.29e-06	7.205	0.00051	1.87e-06	3.301
VOL											
count ≥ 20	24	1.0005	1538.9	[0, 1]	1842	1.0003	2.72e-05	1864	1.0003	7.82e-03	1856
PACK											
totalWeight ≥ 4	1132	0.95051	54	[0.95051, 1]	24	0.95038	1.00e-06	126.2	0.95046	1.12e-06	123.89

Table 6.7.: Comparison of `NProbability`, `VolComp`, `qCoral` and our approach

Method	Branch Location	# PCs	[1 ... 10]	[1 ... 50]	[1 ... 100]
add	1	7	6.1218×10^{-2}	6.4499×10^{-2}	6.8939×10^{-2}
	2	10	3.3261×10^{-1}	3.5542×10^{-1}	3.7677×10^{-1}
	3	7	6.1218×10^{-2}	6.4499×10^{-2}	6.8939×10^{-2}
	4	10	3.3261×10^{-1}	3.5542×10^{-1}	3.7677×10^{-1}
delete	5	7	4.3999×10^{-1}	4.7931×10^{-1}	4.9165×10^{-1}
	6	14	3.5834×10^{-1}	3.7464×10^{-1}	3.8802×10^{-1}
	7	14	5.3759×10^{-2}	5.7464×10^{-2}	6.1537×10^{-2}
	8	1	0.9399×10^{-6}	2.4310×10^{-7}	1.3728×10^{-9}

Table 6.8.: Probability for covering branches in a Binary Search Tree

Coverage Probability and Program Understanding: The following experiments are conducted on a Binary Tree implementation with a correct implementation of the method delete as proposed by [90]. The implementation can be found in the Appendix and in [77]. We want to examine how the probability of covering a certain program location changes when changing the input values. We used our approach to compute the probability of reaching different branches in the code implementing the methods `add(n)` and `delete(n)`. The source code can be found in Appendix. Both methods take integer values as input. We bounded the scope input domain to data structures with 3 nodes with increasing data value ranges $[1 \ldots 10]$, $[1 \ldots 50]$ and $[1 \ldots 100]$. We compute for different branches in the code all path conditions that reach the branch as well as their probabilities. The probability of the branch is approximated by the sum of the probabilities of the path conditions reaching it. The results are presented in Table 6.8. The probabilities are rounded for presentation purposes. The Branch Location column indicates the location in the code, # PCs refers to how many path conditions reach the branch and the three following columns show the computed probability to reach the branch. The parameter values are chosen uniform randomly from the intervals.

First observation to make is that there is no correlation between the number of path conditions reaching a branch and the probability of covering that branch. For example, the branch at location 7 of method `delete` is reached by 14 PCs and the probability to cover it is smaller than the branch at location 7 which is reached by only 7 PCs. Considering the implementation code of the method `add`, the branches at locations 1 and 3 as well as the branches at location 2 and 4 are symmetric around the check whether the value to add is less or greater than current root value. This code aspect is captured by our probabilistic approach.

Next observation we can make is that for some branches the probability to reach them increases when the range of value increases. For example, adding values to the binary tree is easier when the range of values to select from is larger: it is less likely to select and add a value that is already in the binary tree. The branch at location 8 in the method `delete` is the least likely to be reached. This event becomes more rare when the range of allowed input values increases. Based on the implementation code, this branch corresponds to the case when we try to delete the root node when the tree is empty. This is an unlikely behavior since it simulates deleting an element from an empty tree.

Scalability Remarks: Korat enumerates each possible data structure including all input values. Such an enumeration can be very expensive especially when the range of possible input values increases. For counting data structure models with values in [1 . . . 10], Korat took less than 2 seconds on average. However, for values in the range [1 . . . 50] Korat took 17 minutes and more than 2 hours on average for values in the range [1 . . . 100].

Probability of a Bug: For the next set of experiments we study the probability of triggering the bug reported by [90] under different operational profiles. We use the buggy implementation which can be found in [77]. The code has a bug in the `delete` method. The bug makes it impossible to remove the root element of the tree and sometimes incorrectly deletes subtrees [90]. We limit the data values in the container to the range [1...50] and perform the calls `add` and `delete` randomly. We evaluate sequences of 7 calls after which we check whether the bug was triggered by using an assertion.

The operational profile as shown in Table 6.9 vary the probability of performing the calls and the probability of choosing the values. The first scenario considers the case where both the calls and the inputs are selected uniformly from their domains (i.e. each with 0.5 probability). The second and the third scenarios consider respectively the cases where 70 % of the time `delete` is called and where only 30 % of the time `delete` is called. This follows the intuition that the bug is in the `delete` method. However, in fact the more we delete the less will be the probability to trigger the bug. This means that the execution of the buggy code region is related to how and when `delete` is called. This is justified by the two last scenarios where no `delete` is called last and where the last two calls are not a `delete` call in the sequence (the probability to trigger the bug is zero).

Calls Distribution	Values Distribution	Probability to trigger the bug
Uniform	Uniform	0.000 641
70 % `delete`	Uniform	0.001 13
30 % `delete`	Uniform	0.008 26
No `delete` in the last call	Uniform	0.001 63
No `delete` in the last two calls	Uniform	0

Table 6.9.: Probability of triggering a bug in a the Binary Tree

6.2.3. Reliability Estimation Efficiency and Accuracy

In order to compare the efficiency of the white-box reliability assessment approach with the black-box one, we conduct several experiments on two software artifacts. We compare then for each approach the number of test cases required until reaching a target confidence level and margin of error. For all two artifacts, we assume a uniform operational profile, where we divide the definition domain into two equally probable sub-domains. The artifacts are the following:

- MER: models a component of the flight software for JPL Mars Exploration Rovers (MER) [5]. It consists of a resource arbiter an two other components competing for five resources. MER has 4697 LOC including the Polyglot framework.
- Windy: a standard example from the reinforcement learning literature; a robot, affected by wind, moves in a grid with start and target positions. We analyze two versions: simple ($5x4$ grid) and complex ($9x6$ grid) [61].

$1-\alpha$	d	# testcases	
		Black-Box	White-Box
0.99	10^{-2}	12028	10351
0.99	10^{-3}	13089	12804
0.99	10^{-4}	16293	14618

(a) MER(small)#path: 122

$1-\alpha$	d	#testcases	
		Black-Box	White-Box
0.99	10^{-2}	13082	6297
0.99	10^{-3}	14762	6845
0.99	10^{-4}	14914	6938

(b) Windy(small) #path: 614

Table 6.10.: White-Box Reliability Assessment v.s. Black-box Reliability Assessment

The software artifacts contain injected faults for the purpose of testing [5]. MER contains one known fault, Windy contains 3 faults.

Table 6.10 summarizes the number of test cases required by each technique (i.e, black-box and white-box) to reach a target confidence level and margin of error. Here, we do not repair faults if failures are revealed.

Table 6.10 confirms the mathematical theory of stratified sampling. Since the white-box reliability assessment approach considers each path condition as a sub-domain, then it will decrease systematically the variance of the reliability estimate. The black-box approach divides, however, the test cases over only two sub-domains. Another observation is: when we decrease the margin of error, the required number of test cases to reach the confidence goal, for both approaches does not vary too much. We explain this phenomena with the fact that our both approaches are designed to systematically reduce the variance of the estimate.

6.3. Verification-based Reliability Assessment

The goal of this section is to show the applicability of the verification-based reliability assessment approach in the following two scenarios:

1. when a proof attempt succeeds, i.e., all proof obligations are closed: all path conditions are verified as correct with regard to a formal specification
2. when a proof tree fails, i.e., some proof obligations remain open: only some path conditions (but not all) are verified as correct.

6.4. Implementation Details

The prototype implementation uses the KeY system to extract the symbolically executed proof obligations. Each proof obligation is then represented by a path condition. Based on a given operational profile, we compute the probability of each path condition using our tool for probabilistic program analysis (see section 6.2.1).

In order to generate JUnit test cases, we use the tool Korat.

6.5. Experiment Subject

We use for this validation a standard KeY example, a banking example code, which implements the following three methods

1. Bank.login(userdid, password)
2. UserAccount.getBankAccount(num)
3. UserAccount.tryLogin(userid, password)

We assessed the reliability of the method UserAccount.tryLogin using our black-box approach. Each call of the method UserAccount.tryLogin is annotated with its reliability and corresponding variance.

Our goal now is to assess the reliability of the methods Bank.login and UserAccount.getBankAccount using the verification-based approach. We assume that the execution environment has an availability of 0.9

We define an operational profile for our reliability assessment scenario using the following two parameters:

1. numus : the number of user accounts
2. numacc : the number of bank accounts

We defined the operational profile for this scenario as follows:

1. Scenario 1 : numus in [0, 3000], numacc in [0, 7500]: 40 %
2. Scenario 2 : numus in [3000, 6000], numacc in [7500, 18000]: 60 %

Both methods are formally verified using KeY. Table 6.11 lists the simplified path conditions of the method Bank.login with their probabilities.

Table 6.13 lists the simplified path conditions of the method getBankAccount.

When All Path Conditions Verified In this case, the reliability of each method is defined as presented in Section 5.5 as:

$$\hat{R} = \sum_{i=1}^{3} \mathbb{P}(PC_i^c|OP).(1 - FR_i)$$

For example, the reliability of the method Bank.login is estimated as follows:

$$R_{login} = 0.37 * \mu(\text{try}\hat{\text{L}}\text{ogin}) * 0.9 + 0.11 * 0.9 + 0.52 * 0.9$$

index	Path Conditions	Probability
1	userid >= 0, userid < numus	0.37
2	userid <0	0.11
3	userid >= 0, userid > numus	0.52

Table 6.11.: Path Conditions and their Probabilities- `Bank.login`

Index	Path Conditions	Probability	verified?
1	userid >= 0, userid + 500 <numus	0.31	verified
2	userid <0	0.11	verified
3	userid >= 0, userid + 500 >= numus	0.58	n.a

Table 6.12.: Path Conditions and their Probabilities after Fault Injection- `Bank.login`

When Some Path Conditions are not Verified We inject some faults in both methods. The obtained results are illustrated in the tables 6.12 and 6.14.

For example, the reliability of the method UserAccount.getBankAccount is:

$$R_{\text{getBankAccount}} = 0.08 * 0.9 + 0.36 * 0.9$$

with a confidence $c = 1 - 0.58$

In this case, the confidence $c = 1 - 0.58$ is too low. In order to increase the confidence, the white-box reliability assessment should be used.

Index	Path Conditions	Probability
1	num <0	0.08
2	num >= 0, numacc >num	0.38
3	num >= 0, num >= numacc	0.52

Table 6.13.: Path Conditions and their Probabilities - `UserAccount.getBankAccount`

Index	Path Conditions	Probabilities	verified?
1	num <0	0.08	verified
2	num >= 0, num + 500 <numacc	0.36	verified
3	num >= 0, num + 500 >= numacc	0.56	n.a

Table 6.14.: Path Conditions and their Probabilities after Fault Injection - `UserAccount.getBankAccount`

6.6. Sensitivity Analysis

Software statistical testing characterizes the field of use of the tested software using an operational profile. Determining an operational profile can be difficult in practice and might introduce some errors when estimating it. We conduct a sensitivity analysis to investigate the effect of an error in the operational profile on the change of the reliability estimate variance.

The sensitivity value of an error in the operational profile is computed based on the analytical approach presented in [68]. Let $\mathcal{D}_j$ be the sub-domain whose probability is in error, and let $\varepsilon_{\mathcal{D}_j}$ be the error in probability. We use the subscript F to indicate quantities associated with the true operational profile in field use and T to indicate erroneous quantities associated with the testing operational profile. Then $\varepsilon_{\mathcal{D}_j} = p_{T_{\mathcal{D}_j}} - p_{F_{\mathcal{D}_j}}$, where $p_{T_{\mathcal{D}_j}}$ the estimated probability of occurrence of $\mathcal{D}_j$ used when testing and $p_{F_{\mathcal{D}_j}}$ the true probability of occurrence. Since probabilities can vary between 0 and 1, it follows: $-p_{F_{\mathcal{D}_j}} \leq \varepsilon_{\mathcal{D}_j} \leq 1 - p_{F_{\mathcal{D}_j}}$. Let $\eta_{\mathcal{D}_j}$ be the relative error defined as $\eta_{\mathcal{D}_j} = \varepsilon_{\mathcal{D}_j}/p_{F_{\mathcal{D}_j}}$. Then $-1 \leq \eta_{\mathcal{D}_j} \leq (1/p_{F_{\mathcal{D}_j}} - 1)$. Since we only select tests from sub-domains specified in the operational profile, the sum of the probabilities $p_{F_{\mathcal{D}_j}}$ and $p_{T_{\mathcal{D}_j}}$ for the operational profile sub-domains are both 1. Consequently, the sum of errors $\varepsilon_{\mathcal{D}_k}$ over the sub-domains must be 0 [68]. Therefore, the existence of the error $\varepsilon_{\mathcal{D}_j}$ implies the existence of other errors in probability or difference between the test and field operational profiles $\varepsilon_{\mathcal{D}_k}$ that are nonzero. There are no known factors that would cause $\varepsilon_{\mathcal{D}_j}$ to affect the other $\varepsilon_{\mathcal{D}_k}$. Hence, we can assume that all $\varepsilon_{\mathcal{D}_k}$ are affected in the same relative way so they have the same relative error η. Since the sum the probabilities of occurrence is equal 1, we obtain

$$\frac{\eta = -\eta_{\mathcal{D}_j} . p_{F_{\mathcal{D}_j}}}{(1 - p_{F_{\mathcal{D}_j}})}$$

Consequently, an error in one occurrence probability of the operational profile causes errors in other probabilities of occurrence. The sensitivity of the reliability estimator variance on an error in the probability of occurrence of a sub-domain $\mathcal{D}_i$ can be then defined as the ratio of of relative errors for the variances as follows:

$$\frac{\mathcal{S}_{\mathcal{D}_j} = (\frac{\text{var}_T - \text{var}_F}{\text{var}_F})}{\eta_{\mathcal{D}_j}} \tag{6.1}$$

The goal of our white-box reliability assessment approach is to generate fine-grained sub-domains, which even if they are not truly homogeneous, they are usually less heterogeneous than the original sub-domains. Consequently, if an error in the probability of a sub-domain occurs, it might not affect the variance significantly. Since the total variance of the reliability estimate is defined as $\text{var}[\widehat{R}] = \sum_{i=1}^{L} {p_i}^2 \frac{{\sigma_i}^2}{n_i}$, then an error in the probability of a sub-domain would lead to small variations of $\frac{\text{var}_T - \text{var}_F}{\text{var}_F}$. Consequently, when our white-box approach is used, then the sensitivity will tend to zero.

Asymptotically, our black-box approach would reduce the variance within each sub-domain through extra testing. So asymptotically, the black-box approach would be able to reduce the sensitivity of the reliability estimation to variations of the operational profile.

The verification-based approach is able to reduce the input domain of the software since it does not execute path conditions verified as correct. The reduction of the input domain reduces the probability to introduce errors when estimating the probabilities of the operational profile sub-domains.

7. Related Work

This chapter highlights existing approaches and addresses the relationship to our work.

7.1. Statistical Testing based on Sampling

Stratified sampling is linked to the idea of partition testing or sub-domain testing of a software.

In [50] and [95], partition testing is compared to simple random sampling from a program's input domain with respect to the probability of detecting at least one failure during testing. Inputs were selected randomly from each partition. Different combinations of partition size, partition probability of occurrence, partition failure rate and overall failure rate were considered. [50] and [95] conclude that partition testing is significantly more effective than random testing when one ore more partition have a relative high failure rate. Our approach is aligned with the conclusions of [50] and [95]. since the program failure rates are usually not known in advance, it is safer to use partition testing instead of simple random testing to assess the failure rate of a program. Our approach adaptively selects inputs from each partition, more inputs are selected from the partitions which have a relative observed high failure rate. In addition, our approach considers the probability of occurrence of each partition by adaptively selecting inputs towards a 100% similarity to the operational profile probabilities.

[88] present the usage of probabilistic test generation for fault detection. They generate automatically tests to address different behavioral and structural test criteria. Apparently, in [88], they view the evaluation of tests as *inexpensive*. They call their approach "statistical testing" although it dos not involve reliability estimation. In contrast to [88], we think that evaluating test is an

expensive process. Our approach aims to reduce the variance of a reliability estimator and consequently reduce the required number of executed and evaluated test cases to reach a target reliability confidence.

Techniques to estimate software reliability using partition testing, which resemble conventional stratified sampling, are proposed in [14], [34] and [70] for example. They introduced the idea of sampling to reliability estimation but did not specify a sampling design. To account for operational profile, [14] present a stratified reliability estimator similar to the reliability estimator (see equation 3.4) we present in our approach. They assume that the estimator is unbiased, when all sub-domains are sampled using simple random sampling within the entire program's input domain. This assumption is repeated in [76]. This assumption is incorrect however: the estimator is generally biased unless we further assume that all possible inputs are equally likely to arise in operational use. ([14] and [76] do not make such an assumption.)

[65] present a stratified estimator of the the failure rate when no failures occur during testing by incorporating prior assumptions about the failure rate in the estimation. They reuse the approach presented in [14] and they do not consider the variance of the estimator.

The work of [75] is related to our research. However, they only used the idea of equal stratification using clustering to estimate the software reliability from software execution profiles collected by capture/replay tools. Failure rates have been extensively used in the area of adaptive random testing ([16], [19], [56]). Adaptive random testing aims to distribute the selected test cases as spaced out as possible to increase the chance of hitting the failure patterns. The intuition behind adaptive random sampling can be added in a future work to our approach to probably further enhance the efficiency of the reliability estimator. [16], [19], [56] do not address the problem of reliability estimator efficiency. A recent work on adaptive testing [54], allocates test cases using a gradient search method based on the variance variation of the failure rate. However, their approach introduces bias resulting from the use of the gradient method: it is possible that all test cases are selected from the sub-domain that first reveals a failure. They avoid such situations by introducing a biased estimator using Bayesian estimation. Consequently, their reliability estimator, in contrast to our estimator, is biased. Contrary to [54], we adopt a global optimization scheme for test cases selection which guarantees that our approach converges to globally optimal solution as testing proceeds.

Furthermore, the approach presented in [54] does not generate test cases which are conform the probabilities of the operational profile sub-domains, which would further bias the reliability estimate.

[58] developed a Bayesian-based stopping criteria for statistical testing. In contrast to the stopping criteria presented in [58], our approach does not use uniform prior but updates the prior after test execution. Furthermore, our stopping criteria allows to specify a margin of error in addition to the required confidence level as a stopping criteria. In addition, the stopping criteria in [58], in opposition to our approach is not designed with setting to distribute the test cases across the operational profile sub-domains, or to consider the failure rate of the different sub-domains.

7.2. Combining Statistical Testing with Formal Verification

[28] presents a transformational approach for the assessment of software reliability. The main idea of [28] is to apply vertical slicing to reduce the dimension of the software input domain, and horizontal slicing to reduce the cardinality of the input domain. The reduction of the input domain is achieved through the verification of the slices. The goal of the combination of formal verification and statistical testing is to reduce the amount of testing required to attain a target confidence level on the reliability estimate. However, in contrast to our approach, [28] makes no quantitative statements about the gain of using formal verification, does not define how the software reliability will be computed in the presence of formal proofs. Furthermore, [28] abstracts from the execution environment and assumes that proved program slices do not need to be tested. However, such an assumption is very misleading. Our approach, however, is able to analyze the reliability of a software program in an execution environment. The approach in [28] is actually not a combination of formal verification and statistical testing, rather formal verification has been used to reduce the input domain of software programs and hence reduce the testing effort usually required by statistical testing.

Another work [27] accelerates statistical testing by applying monotonic transformations to the software program and the execution environment (e.g., program slicing, replacing function computation by table lookup, use of fast process simulation or use of centralized instead of distributed computing). Such transformations imply the correctness of the original program, and a failure of the transformed program does not necessary means that the original program would fail. This would require the invocation and test of the original version. In addition, the approach presented in [27] is labor-intensive requiring the formal verification of each transformation by skilled software engineers, which would limit the applicability of the approach.

7.3. Software Reliability Modeling and Prediction

The goal of Software Reliability Growth Models is to describe the software failure process in form of a stochastic process. The stochastic process is usually used for software reliability prediction and estimation. Software reliability growth models assume that faults repair is made on the go as testing progress, and that the faults repair results in decreasing failure rate.

Software reliability growth models received much attention with more than 100 different models [62]. However, the usage of software reliability growth models require usually assumptions, which are questionable and sometime unrealistic [62], [2].

Therefore, many research solution has been presented to address the assumptions related to software reliability growth models such as applying time series models, especially ARIMA models like [2]. However, such models require timed failure data, which is usually not always available. Furthermore, in contrast to our non-parametric Gaussian process model, such models provide no measure of the uncertainty of the prediction. In addition, the usage of such models requires special attention to satisfy the assumptions of the time series models.

A recent work [89], presents a Gaussian process failure count prediction model using software metrics as independent variables. [89] generates one single model for the whole software and do not account for the number of test cases executions. The generated model is trained on existing data to predict future behavior. Our approach, however, generates a model for each sub-domain of the failure. One main advantage of generating a Gaussian process for each sub-domain is as follows: each Gaussian process models a different subspace of the input domain, which allows learning multimodal data distribution with more flexibility than a single model for the input domain. Furthermore, our model is trained adaptively (only when needed), based on the uncertainty provided by the prediction. Another recent work [17], predicts failure count using Bayesian-based support vector machines, where the independent variables are software metrics as in [89]. Like [89], the approach in [17] is not designed to adaptively train itself based on the prediction uncertainty. Our prediction model makes effective use of previous test executions during model inference. Based on the uncertainty on the prediction and confidence goals on the reliability estimate and cost constraints, the approach decides whether to execute the test cases or not.

7.4. Probabilistic Program Analysis

Our white-box reliability assessment approach is related to many areas including statistical model checking [52], analysis of probabilistic programs [66], and integration methods over polyhedras [30]. We compute the probability of a path condition or more generally a set of path conditions that lead to a program behavior of interest. The techniques for the probability computation of the path conditions differ in the approach used to approximate the solution space, the distribution type of the input variables and the linearity of the constraints.

Geldenhuys et al. [39] present an approach that considers only uniform distributed input variables and linear integer arithmetic constraints. They used LattE Machiato [30] to count the solution space of the path conditions. One main difference between this work and ours is that we support complex nonlinear constraints and we use constraint propagation techniques to approximate the solution space. In addition our approach is not restricted to uniform distribution. The approach of Geldenhuys et al., in contrast to our approach, do not handle symbolic data structures. They assume that the structures are concrete and only the data is symbolic. In our approach both the input structure as well as the input data is taken to be symbolic. Sankaranarayanan et al. [81] recently proposed a technique to remove the restriction of uniform distribution by developing an algorithm for the under and over-approximation of probabilities. They use Linear Programming solvers to compute the over-approximations and heuristics to compute the under-approximation. However, their approach is limited to linear constraints. More recently, Borges et al. [11] proposed an approach for handling nonlinear constraints based on interval constraint propagation techniques and Monte Carlo integration. One main technical difference between this approach and our work is that our approach is incremental and computes probabilities at each branching constraint which allows for better scalability of symbolic execution. The approach of Borges et al. computes the probabilities after symbolic execution finishes. In addition, our work extends interval constraint propagation by allowing to control the efficiency of the solution space approximation. The approximation procedure is controlled based on a user-defined accuracy parameter on the computed probability of a target program behavior. Furthermore, our work makes use of the joint box cover structure computed by the interval constraint propagation techniques and applies Monte Carlo integration only on the outer cover. Borges et al. apply Monte Carlo integration on the whole approximated solution space. Consequently, their approach as shown in our experiments may require more samples to compute the probabilities with a given accuracy. Moreover, our work supports constraints over data structure which is not supported by Borges et al.

8. Conclusion

Our society rely on the correct functioning of software systems and our dependence on them is growing. The failure of software systems can be disastrous resulting in humanitarian and financial damages. Consequently, it is necessary to assess the reliability of software systems with high confidence.

However, existing software reliability assessment techniques are usually either theoretical sound, labor-intensive and time-consuming or practical but not trustworthy because of their underlying unrealistic assumptions and poor estimation accuracy. Therefore, software development organizations are considering software reliability assessment as a cost rather than a return. The reliability of a software is usually assessed using formal verification or testing.

Formal verification can prove perfect reliability of the software. However, it is usually impractical to verify the program as well as its execution environment. Furthermore, if formal verification is applied to only some parts of the software, existing techniques do not account for the confidence gained from verification in the reliability estimate.

Exhaustive testing is usually impossible for complex real world software system. Therefore, statistical testing based on sample models according to an operational profile has been proposed as the theoretical sound tools to assess the software reliability. However, statistical testing requires a large number of test cases to reach a target confidence on the reliability estimate.

This dissertation proposes a solution to reduce the overhead required by statistical testing, and developed a method to account for any formal verification effort in the reliability estimation. In order to reduce the overhead required by statistical testing, we formulated our approach as an uncertainty reduction technique, which aims to use the available information about the software in order to efficiently assess and reduce the uncertainty about the software future behavior. The information can be provided from (i) previous test cases execution, (ii) the source code of the software (iii) previous formal verification attempts. The more information we have about the software under study the more our approach gains on efficiency. In order to account for any formal verification effort, we developed a method to symbolically estimate the software reliability before executing any test cases if the program has been verified even partially. Furthermore, we proposed a novel combination of deductive formal verification with statistical testing.

The main contribution of this dissertation can be arranged in three groups.

First, we developed a black-box reliability assessment approach which adaptively sample test cases from the sub-domains of an operational profile. The approach learns from previous test cases executions and computes in an iterative manner the required number of test cases to be executed based on user required confidence level. Compared to state-of-the-art approaches, we could reach a target confidence with less test cases. Furthermore, we developed a non-parametric reliability prediction model based on Gaussian process. The model is trained adaptively, and decides at each iteration to predict the future failure rate or to execute the test cases.

The second contribution is white-box reliability assessment, which makes use of the source code information to generate based on the operational profile sub-domains finer partitions. The finer partitions are then used as the new sub-domains. This required the development of a probabilistic symbolic execution engine. The novel symbolic execution engine propagates the uncertain information provided by the operational profile while executing the source code symbolically. If in addition to the operational profile, the source code if available, our approach benefits from the white-box information available to further enhance the efficiency of the black-box approach. We developed an automated probabilistic analysis approach of source code based on symbolic execution. The white-box approach propagates the uncertain information provided by the operational profile while executing the source code symbolically. Compared to the black-box approach, the white-box approach makes use of the source code information to further reduce the number of required test cases to reach a target statistical confidence on the reliability estimate.

The third contribution is verification-based reliability assessment which merges the strengths of both formal verification and statistical testing in a coherent form. The reliability estimate is derived from the proof tree. If the reliability goal cannot be reached by symbolic computation of the reliability, the approach complements the reliability estimate by test cases derived from the open proof branches. The test cases are derived using the white-box reliability assessment approach. The developed approach analyzes the reliability of a program in a runtime environment without explicitly modeling the environment in the verification logic.

The stopping criteria of our approach does not consider the case when a fault repair introduces new faults. A possible improvement of our approach is to develop models for fault-repair. Our prototype tool implementation for the verification-based reliability assessment is using Korat for the generation of the JUnit test cases. KeY can however efficiently generate test cases for open proof obligations toward fault detection. Our approach can benefit from such capabilities. We also plan to investigate further applications of the probabilistic symbolic execution approach in the analysis of Cyber physical systems, or code-based security analysis. Idea of the probabilistic bound which guides the symbolic execution can be used in the context of bounded verification to systematically increase the bound when needed.

A. Appendix

This appendix presents the code for the Binary Search Tree example used in this thesis.

A.1. Implementation Code of the Method add

```
public void add(int x) {
    Node current = root;

    if (root == null) {
      root = new Node(x);
      return;
    }

    while (current.value != x) {
      if (current.value > x) {
        if (current.left == null) {
          //Location 1
          current.left = new Node(x);
        } else {
          //Location 2
          current = current.left;
        }
      } else {
        if (current.right == null) {
          //Location 3
          current.right = new Node(x);
        } else {
          //Location 4
          current = current.right;
```

```
            }
         }
      }
   }
```

A.2. Implementation Code of the Method delete

```
public boolean delete(int x) {
     Node current = root;
     Node parent = root;

     boolean isLeftChild = true;

     if (current == null)
       return false;

     while(current.value != x) {
       //assign parent to current
       parent = current;
       if(current.value > x) {
         //Location 5
           isLeftChild = true;
           current = current.left;
        }
       else {
         //Location 6
           isLeftChild = false;
           current = current.right;
        }
       if(current == null) {
         //Location 7
         return false;
       }
     }

    if(current.left == null && current.right == null) {
       if(current == root) {
       //Location 8
       root = null;
       }
       else if(isLeftChild) {
        parent.left = null;
     }
       else {
       parent.right = null;
```

```
      }
    }
    else if(current.right == null)
      if(current == root) {
        root = current.left;
      }
      else if(isLeftChild) {
        parent.left = current.left;
      }
      else {
        parent.right = current.left;
      }
    else if(current.left == null)
      if(current == root) {
        root = current.right;
      }
      else if(isLeftChild) {
        parent.left = current.right;
      }
      else {
        parent.right = current.right;
      }

    else {

      Node successor = getSuccessor(current);

      if(current == root) {
        root = successor;
      }
      else if(isLeftChild) {
        parent.left= successor;
      }
       else {
        parent.right = successor;
       }

      successor.left = current.left;
     }
    return true;
}
```

Bibliography

[1] *Airbus A400M: Der Katastrophenflieger.* Online; accessed 01-June-2015. URL: http://www.spiegel.de/wissenschaft/technik/airbus-a400m-absturz-tiefpunkt-eines-fehlerbehafteten-projekts-a-1033011.html (cit. on p. 3).

[2] A. Amin, L. Grunske, and A. Colman. „An approach to software reliability prediction based on time series modeling.“ In: *Journal of Systems and Software* 86.7 (2013), pp. 1923–1932 (cit. on p. 142).

[3] J. H. Andrews, L. C. Briand, and Y. Labiche. „Is Mutation an Appropriate Tool for Testing Experiments?“ In: *Proceedings of the 27th International Conference on Software Engineering.* ICSE '05. St. Louis, MO, USA: ACM, 2005, pp. 402–411 (cit. on p. 122).

[4] ANSI/IEEE. „Standard Glossary of Software Engineering Terminology.“ In: *STD-729-1991* (1991) (cit. on pp. 2, 15).

[5] D. Balasubramanian, C. S. Păsăreanu, G. Karsai, and M. R. Lowry. „Polyglot: Systematic Analysis for Multiple Statechart Formalisms.“ English. In: *Tools and Algorithms for the Construction and Analysis of Systems.* Ed. by N. Piterman and S. Smolka. Vol. 7795. Lecture Notes in Computer Science. Springer Berlin Heidelberg, 2013, pp. 523–529 (cit. on pp. 132, 133).

[6] B. Beckert and C. Gladisch. „White-box Testing by Combining Deduction-based Specification Extraction and Black-box Testing.“ In: *Proceedings of the 1st International Conference on Tests and Proofs.* TAP'07. Zurich, Switzerland: Springer-Verlag, 2007, pp. 207–216 (cit. on p. 5).

[7] B. Beckert, R. Hähnle, and P. H. Schmitt, eds. *Verification of Object-Oriented Software: The KeY Approach.* LNCS 4334. Springer-Verlag, 2007 (cit. on p. 46).

[8] B. Beckert, R. Hähnle, and P. H. Schmitt. *Verification of Object-oriented Software: The KeY Approach.* Berlin, Heidelberg: Springer-Verlag, 2007 (cit. on p. 5).

[9] F. Benhamou, F. Goualard, L. Granvilliers, and J.-F. Puget. „Revising Hull and Box Consistency." In: *Proceedings of the 1999 International Conference on Logic Programming.* Las Cruces, New Mexico, USA: Massachusetts Institute of Technology, 1999, pp. 230–244 (cit. on pp. 89, 90).

[10] F. Benhamou and W. J. Older. „Applying interval arithmetic to real, integer and Boolean constraints." In: *JOURNAL OF LOGIC PROGRAMMING* 32.1 (1997), pp. 1–24 (cit. on pp. 89, 92).

[11] M. Borges, A. Filieri, M. d'Amorim, C. S. Păsăreanu, and W. Visser. „Compositional Solution Space Quantification for Probabilistic Software Analysis." In: *SIGPLAN Not.* 49.6 (June 2014) (cit. on pp. 127, 144).

[12] C. Boyapati, S. Khurshid, and D. Marinov. „Korat: Automated Testing Based on Java Predicates." In: *SIGSOFT Softw. Eng. Notes* 27.4 (July 2002), pp. 123–133 (cit. on p. 92).

[13] F. Brosch, H. Koziolek, B. Buhnova, and R. Reussner. „Architecture-Based Reliability Prediction with the Palladio Component Model." In: *Software Engineering, IEEE Transactions on* 38.6 (Nov. 2012), pp. 1319–1339 (cit. on pp. 3, 28, 30).

[14] J. R. Brown and M. Lipow. „Testing for Software Reliability." In: *SIGPLAN Not.* 10.6 (Apr. 1975), pp. 518–527 (cit. on p. 140).

[15] R. W. Butler and G. B. Finelli. „The Infeasibility of Quantifying the Reliability of Life-Critical Real-Time Software." In: *IEEE Trans. Softw. Eng.* 19.1 (Jan. 1993), pp. 3–12 (cit. on pp. 1, 6, 10).

[16] J. W. CANGUSSU, K. COOPER, and W. E. WONG. „A segment based approach for the reduction of the number of test cases for performance evaluation of components." In: *International Journal of Software Engineering and Knowledge Engineering* 19.04 (2009), pp. 481–505. eprint: `http://www.worldscientific.com/doi/pdf/10.1142/S0218194009004283` (cit. on p. 140).

[17] S. Chatzis and A. Andreou. „Maximum Entropy Discrimination Poisson Regression for Software Reliability Modeling." In: *Neural Networks and Learning Systems, IEEE Transactions on* PP.99 (2015), pp. 1–1 (cit. on p. 143).

[18] M.-H. Chen, A. Mathur, and V. Rego. „A case study to investigate sensitivity of reliability estimates to errors in operational profile." In: *Software Reliability Engineering, 1994. Proceedings., 5th International Symposium on.* Nov. 1994, pp. 276–281 (cit. on p. 24).

[19] T. Y. Chen, F.-C. Kuo, R. G. Merkel, and T. H. Tse. „Adaptive Random Testing: The ART of Test Case Diversity." In: *J. Syst. Softw.* 83.1 (Jan. 2010), pp. 60–66 (cit. on p. 140).

[20] T. Y. Chen and Y. T. Yu. „On the expected number of failures detected by subdomain testing and random testing." In: *Software Engineering, IEEE Transactions on* 22.2 (Feb. 1996), pp. 109–119 (cit. on p. 27).

[21] S. Chidamber and C. Kemerer. „A metrics suite for object oriented design." In: *Software Engineering, IEEE Transactions on* 20.6 (June 1994), pp. 476–493 (cit. on p. 123).

[22] W. Cochran. *Sampling techniques.* Wiley series in probability and mathematical statistics: Applied probability and statistics. Wiley, 1977 (cit. on pp. 39, 41).

[23] E. Cohen, M. Dahlweid, M. Hillebrand, D. Leinenbach, M. Moskal, T. Santen, W. Schulte, and S. Tobies. „VCC: A Practical System for Verifying Concurrent C." In: *Proceedings of the 22Nd International Conference on Theorem Proving in Higher Order Logics.* TPHOLs '09. Munich, Germany: Springer-Verlag, 2009, pp. 23–42 (cit. on p. 5).

[24] D. R. Cok and J. R. Kiniry. „ESC/Java2: Uniting ESC/Java and JML - Progress and issues in building and using ESC/Java2." In: *In Construction and Analysis of Safe, Secure and Interoperable Smart Devices: International Workshop, CASSIS 2004.* Springer?Verlag, 2004 (cit. on p. 5).

[25] A. Crespo, P. Matrella, and A. Pasquini. „Sensitivity of reliability growth models to operational profile errors." In: *Software Reliability Engineering, 1996. Proceedings., Seventh International Symposium on.* Oct. 1996, pp. 35–44 (cit. on p. 24).

[26] B. Cukic and F. Bastani. „On reducing the sensitivity of software reliability to variations in the operational profile." In: *Software Reliability Engineering, 1996. Proceedings., Seventh International Symposium on.* Oct. 1996, pp. 45–54 (cit. on p. 8).

[27] B. Cukic. „Accelerated Testing for Software Reliability Assessment." In: (1990) (cit. on pp. 7, 8, 141, 142).

[28] B. Cukic. „Combining testing and correctness verification in software reliability assessment." In: *High-Assurance Systems Engineering Workshop, 1997., Proceedings.* Aug. 1997, pp. 182–187 (cit. on p. 141).

[29] M. D'Ambros, M. Lanza, and R. Robbes. „An extensive comparison of bug prediction approaches." In: *Mining Software Repositories (MSR), 2010 7th IEEE Working Conference on.* May 2010, pp. 31–41 (cit. on pp. 122, 123).

[30] J. A. De Loera, B. Dutra, M. Köppe, S. Moreinis, G. Pinto, and J. Wu. „Software for Exact Integration of Polynomials over Polyhedra." In: *ACM Commun. Comput. Algebra* 45.3/4 (Jan. 2012), pp. 169–172 (cit. on p. 143).

[31] L. De Moura and N. Bjørner. „Z3: An Efficient SMT Solver." In: *Proceedings of the Theory and Practice of Software, 14th International Conference on Tools and Algorithms for the Construction and Analysis of Systems.* TACAS'08/ETAPS'08. Budapest, Hungary: Springer-Verlag, 2008, pp. 337–340 (cit. on pp. 5, 46).

[32] H. Do and G. Rothermel. „On the Use of Mutation Faults in Empirical Assessments of Test Case Prioritization Techniques." In: *IEEE Trans. Softw. Eng.* 32.9 (Sept. 2006), pp. 733–752 (cit. on p. 122).

[33] J. W. Duran and S. Ntafos. „An Evaluation of Random Testing." In: *Software Engineering, IEEE Transactions on* SE-10.4 (July 1984), pp. 438–444 (cit. on p. 78).

[34] J. W. Duran and J. J. Wiorkowski. „Quantifying Software Validity by Sampling." In: *Reliability, IEEE Transactions on* R-29.2 (June 1980), pp. 141–144 (cit. on p. 140).

[35] M.-A. El Aroui and C. Lavergne. „Generalized linear models in software reliability: parametric and semi-parametric approaches." In: *Reliability, IEEE Transactions on* 45.3 (Sept. 1996), pp. 463–470 (cit. on p. 123).

[36] N. E. Fenton and S. L. Pfleeger. *Software Metrics: A Rigorous and Practical Approach.* 2nd. Boston, MA, USA: PWS Publishing Co., 1998 (cit. on p. 72).

[37] A. Filieri, C. S. Păsăreanu, and W. Visser. „Reliability Analysis in Symbolic Pathfinder." In: *Proceedings of the 2013 International Conference on Software Engineering.* ICSE '13. San Francisco, CA, USA: IEEE Press, 2013, pp. 622–631 (cit. on p. 7).

[38] J. H. G. Goos. *Software Reliability Modelling and Identification.* 1988 (cit. on p. 21).

[39] J. Geldenhuys, M. B. Dwyer, and W. Visser. „Probabilistic Symbolic Execution." In: *Proceedings of the 2012 International Symposium on Software Testing and Analysis.* ISSTA 2012. Minneapolis, MN, USA: ACM, 2012, pp. 166–176 (cit. on p. 143).

[40] A. Gelman, ed. *Bayesian data analysis.* 2. ed. Texts in statistical science. Boca Raton, Fla. [u.a.]: Chapman and Hall/CRC, 2004 (cit. on pp. 31, 36, 61).

[41] C. Gladisch. „Verification-based Software-fault Detection." PhD thesis. Karlsruhe Institute of Technology (KIT), 2011 (cit. on p. 5).

[42] C. Gladisch, S. Tyszberowicz, B. Beckert, and A. Yehudai. „Generating Regression Unit Tests Using a Combination of Verification and Capture – Replay." In: *Proceedings of the 4th International Conference on Tests and Proofs.* TAP'10. Málaga, Spain: Springer-Verlag, 2010, pp. 61–76 (cit. on p. 5).

[43] A. L. Goel. „Software Reliability Models: Assumptions, Limitations, and Applicability." In: *IEEE Trans. Softw. Eng.* 11.12 (Dec. 1985), pp. 1411–1423 (cit. on p. 21).

[44] A. Goel, R. A. D. Center, S. U. N. Y. D. O. I. ENGINEERING, and O. RESEARCH. *Software Reliability Modelling and Estimation Techniques: Final Technical Report.* RADC-TR-82-263. Defense Technical Information Center, 1982 (cit. on p. 23).

[45] A. L. Goel and K. Okumoto. „An Analysis Of Recurrent Software Errors In A Real-Time Control System." In: *Proceedings of the 1978 Annual Conference.* ACM '78. Washington, D.C., USA: ACM, 1978, pp. 496–501 (cit. on p. 22).

[46] A. L. Goel and K. Okumoto. „Time-Dependent Error-Detection Rate Model for Software Reliability and Other Performance Measures." und. In: *IEEE Transactions on Reliability* R-28.3 (1979), pp. 206–211 (cit. on p. 23).

[47] S. Gokhale, T. Philip, P. Marinos, and K. Trivedi. „Unification of finite failure non-homogeneous Poisson process models through test coverage." In: *Software Reliability Engineering, 1996. Proceedings., Seventh International Symposium on.* Oct. 1996, pp. 299–307 (cit. on p. 24).

[48] L. Granvilliers and F. Benhamou. „RealPaver: An Interval Solver using Constraint Satisfaction Techniques." In: *ACM TRANS. ON MATHEMATICAL SOFTWARE* 32 (2006), pp. 138–156 (cit. on pp. 83, 126).

[49] T. Hall, S. Beecham, D. Bowes, D. Gray, and S. Counsell. „A Systematic Literature Review on Fault Prediction Performance in Software Engineering." In: *Software Engineering, IEEE Transactions on* 38.6 (Nov. 2012), pp. 1276–1304 (cit. on p. 72).

[50] D. Hamlet and R. Taylor. „Partition Testing Does Not Inspire Confidence (Program Testing)." In: *IEEE Trans. Softw. Eng.* 16.12 (Dec. 1990), pp. 1402–1411 (cit. on p. 139).

[51] A. Hassan. „Predicting faults using the complexity of code changes." In: *Software Engineering, 2009. ICSE 2009. IEEE 31st International Conference on.* May 2009, pp. 78–88 (cit. on p. 123).

[52] A. Hinton, M. Kwiatkowska, G. Norman, and D. Parker. „PRISM: A Tool for Automatic Verification of Probabilistic Systems." In: TACAS'06. Vienna, Austria: Springer-Verlag, 2006 (cit. on p. 143).

[53] C. A. R. Hoare. „An Axiomatic Basis for Computer Programming." In: *Commun. ACM* 12.10 (Oct. 1969), pp. 576–580 (cit. on p. 4).

[54] B.-B. y. Junpeng Lv and K.-y. Cai. „On the Asymptotic Behavior of Adaptive Testing Strategy for Software Reliability Assessment." In: *Transaction on software Engineering* (2014) (cit. on pp. 8, 140, 141).

[55] T. M. Khoshgoftaar and N. Seliya. „Fault Prediction Modeling for Software Quality Estimation: Comparing Commonly Used Techniques." In: *Empirical Softw. Engg.* 8.3 (Sept. 2003), pp. 255–283 (cit. on p. 72).

[56] F. C. Kuo, T. Y. Chen, H. Liu, and W. K. Chan. „Enhancing Adaptive Random Testing in High Dimensional Input Domains." In: *Proceedings of the 2007 ACM Symposium on Applied Computing*. SAC '07. Seoul, Korea: ACM, 2007, pp. 1467–1472 (cit. on p. 140).

[57] R. C. Linger. „Cleanroom Software Engineering for Zero-defect Software." In: *Proceedings of the 15th International Conference on Software Engineering*. ICSE '93. Baltimore, Maryland, USA: IEEE Computer Society Press, 1993, pp. 2–13 (cit. on p. 6).

[58] B. Littlewood and D. Wright. „Stopping rules for the operational testing of safety-critical software." In: *Fault-Tolerant Computing, 1995. FTCS-25. Digest of Papers., Twenty-Fifth International Symposium on*. June 1995, pp. 444–451 (cit. on pp. 74, 141).

[59] B. Littlewood and L. Strigini. „Software Reliability and Dependability: A Roadmap." In: *Proceedings of the Conference on The Future of Software Engineering*. ICSE '00. Limerick, Ireland: ACM, 2000, pp. 175–188 (cit. on pp. 2, 4, 9).

[60] B. Littlewood and J. Verrall. „A Bayesian reliability growth model for computer software." In: *Applied statistics* (1973), pp. 332–346 (cit. on p. 22).

[61] K. Luckow, C. S. Păsăreanu, M. B. Dwyer, A. Filieri, and W. Visser. „Exact and Approximate Probabilistic Symbolic Execution for Nondeterministic Programs." In: *Proceedings of the 29th ACM/IEEE International Conference on Automated Software Engineering*. ASE '14. Vasteras, Sweden: ACM, 2014, pp. 575–586 (cit. on p. 132).

[62] M. R. Lyu. „Software Reliability Engineering: A Roadmap." In: *2007 Future of Software Engineering*. FOSE '07. Washington, DC, USA: IEEE Computer Society, 2007, pp. 153–170 (cit. on pp. 1, 142).

[63] *Mathematica, NProbability*. Online; accessed 10-December-2014. URL: `http://reference.wolfram.com/language/ref/NProbability.html` (cit. on p. 127).

[64] B. Meyer. „Design by Contract: Making Object-Oriented Programs that Work." In: *Technology of Object-Oriented Languages and Systems, 1997. TOOLS 25, Proceedings*. Nov. 1997, pp. 360–361 (cit. on p. 4).

[65] K. W. Miller, L. J. Morell, R. E. Noonan, S. K. Park, D. M. Nicol, B. W. Murrill, and J. M. Voas. „Estimating the Probability of Failure When Testing Reveals No Failures." In: *IEEE Trans. Softw. Eng.* 18.1 (Jan. 1992), pp. 33–43 (cit. on p. 140).

[66] D. Monniaux. „An Abstract Monte-Carlo Method for the Analysis of Probabilistic Programs." In: *SIGPLAN Not.* 36.3 (Jan. 2001), pp. 93–101 (cit. on p. 143).

[67] R. E. Moore. *Methods and Applications of Interval Analysis.* 1979, pp. xi + 190 (cit. on p. 89).

[68] J. Musa. „Sensitivity of field failure intensity to operational profile errors." In: *Software Reliability Engineering, 1994. Proceedings., 5th International Symposium on.* Nov. 1994, pp. 334–337 (cit. on p. 137).

[69] J. D. Musa. „Operational Profiles in Software-Reliability Engineering." In: *IEEE Softw.* 10.2 (Mar. 1993), pp. 14–32 (cit. on pp. 6, 8, 18, 19, 48, 114).

[70] E. Nelson. „Estimating software reliability from test data." In: *Microelectronics Reliability* 17.1 (1978), pp. 67–73 (cit. on p. 140).

[71] M. Ohba. „Software Reliability Analysis Models." In: *IBM J. Res. Dev.* 28.4 (Aug. 1984), pp. 428–443 (cit. on p. 24).

[72] F. Omri, S. Omri, and R. Reussner. „Low-Variance Software Reliability Estimation Using Statistical Testing." In: ICSEA '14. Nice, France, 2014, 286 to 292 (cit. on pp. 51, 113).

[73] F. Omri, S. Omri, and R. Reussner. „Incremental and Compositional Probabilistic Program Analysis." In: *Karlsruhe Reports in Informatics ; 2015,2.* 2015 (cit. on pp. 80, 113).

[74] S. Owre, S. Rajan, J. M. Rushby, N. Shankar, and M. Srivas. „PVS: Combining Specification, Proof Checking, and Model Checking." In: Springer-Verlag, 1996, pp. 411–414 (cit. on p. 5).

[75] A. Podgurski, W. Masri, Y. McCleese, F. G. Wolff, and C. Yang. *Estimation of Software Reliability by Stratified Sampling.* 1999 (cit. on p. 140).

[76] A. Podgurski and C. Yang. „Partition Testing, Stratified Sampling, and Cluster Analysis." In: *Proceedings of the 1st ACM SIGSOFT Symposium on Foundations of Software Engineering.* SIGSOFT '93. Los Angeles, California, USA: ACM, 1993, pp. 169–181 (cit. on p. 140).

[77] *Probabilsitic Program Analysis.* URL: https://sdqweb.ipd.kit.edu/wiki/Probabilistic_program_analysis_validation (cit. on pp. 126, 130, 131).

[78] *qCoral.* Online; accessed 10-December-2014. URL: http://pan.cin.ufpe.br/coral/QCORAL.html (cit. on p. 127).

[79] C. V. Ramamoorthy and F. B. Bastani. „Software Reliability Status and Perspectives." In: *IEEE Trans. Softw. Eng.* 8.4 (July 1982), pp. 354–371 (cit. on p. 6).

[80] C. E. Rasmussen and C. K. I. Williams. *Gaussian Processes for Machine Learning (Adaptive Computation and Machine Learning).* The MIT Press, 2005 (cit. on p. 69).

[81] S. Sankaranarayanan, A. Chakarov, and S. Gulwani. „Static Analysis for Probabilistic Programs: Inferring Whole Program Properties from Finitely Many Paths." In: *SIGPLAN Not.* 48.6 (June 2013) (cit. on pp. 127, 143).

[82] G. J. Schick and R. W. Wolverton. „An Analysis of Competing Software Reliability Models." In: *IEEE Trans. Softw. Eng.* 4.2 (Mar. 1978), pp. 104–120 (cit. on p. 22).

[83] E. Schrödinger. „Die gegenwärtige Situation in der Quantenmechanik." German. In: *Naturwissenschaften* 23.49 (1935), pp. 823–828 (cit. on pp. 9, 10).

[84] *Siemens Suite, http://www-static.cc.gatech.edu/aristotle/Tools/subjects.* Feb. 2014. URL: http://www-static.cc.gatech.edu/aristotle/Tools/subjects (cit. on p. 114).

[85] B. Singh and D. L. Parnas. „Estimating Software Reliability Using Inverse Sampling." In: (1997) (cit. on pp. 16, 18).

[86] Y. S. Su, C.-Y. Huang, Y. S. Chen, and J. X. Chen. „An Artificial Neural-Network-Based Approach to Software Reliability Assessment." In: *TENCON 2005 2005 IEEE Region 10.* Nov. 2005, pp. 1–6 (cit. on p. 124).

[87] T. A. Thayer, M. Lipow, and E. C. Nelson. *Software reliability : a study of large project reality.* TRW Series of software technology ; 2. Amsterdam: North-Holland, 1978 (cit. on p. 6).

[88] P. Thévenod-Fosse and H. Waeselynck. „STATEMATE Applied to Statistical Software Testing." In: *Proceedings of the 1993 ACM SIGSOFT International Symposium on Software Testing and Analysis*. ISSTA '93. Cambridge, Massachusetts, USA: ACM, 1993, pp. 99–109 (cit. on p. 139).

[89] N. Torrado, M. Wiper, and R. Lillo. „Software Reliability Modeling with Software Metrics Data via Gaussian Processes." In: *Software Engineering, IEEE Transactions on* 39.8 (Aug. 2013), pp. 1179–1186 (cit. on pp. 142, 143).

[90] W. Visser, J. Geldenhuys, and M. B. Dwyer. „Green: Reducing, Reusing and Recycling Constraints in Program Analysis." In: FSE '12. Cary, North Carolina: ACM, 2012, 58:1–58:11 (cit. on pp. 128, 130, 131).

[91] *VolComp*. Online; accessed 10-December-2014. URL: `http://systems.cs.colorado.edu/research/cyberphysical/probabilistic-program-analysis/` (cit. on p. 127).

[92] S. Wang, Y. Wu, M. Lu, and H. Li. „Software reliability accelerated testing method based on test coverage." In: *Reliability and Maintainability Symposium (RAMS), 2011 Proceedings - Annual*. Jan. 2011, pp. 1–7 (cit. on p. 7).

[93] M. Wenzel, L. Paulson, and T. Nipkow. „The Isabelle Framework." English. In: *Theorem Proving in Higher Order Logics*. Vol. 5170. Lecture Notes in Computer Science. Springer Berlin Heidelberg, 2008, pp. 33–38 (cit. on p. 5).

[94] E. Weyuker and B. Jeng. „Analyzing partition testing strategies." In: *Software Engineering, IEEE Transactions on* 17.7 (July 1991), pp. 703–711 (cit. on p. 78).

[95] E. J. Weyuker and B. Jeng. „Analyzing Partition Testing Strategies." In: *IEEE Trans. Softw. Eng.* 17.7 (July 1991), pp. 703–711 (cit. on p. 139).

[96] L. White and E. Cohen. „A Domain Strategy for Computer Program Testing." In: *Software Engineering, IEEE Transactions on* SE-6.3 (May 1980), pp. 247–257 (cit. on pp. 7, 77, 79).

[97] S. Wilks. *Mathematical Statistics*. Read Books, 2008 (cit. on pp. 31, 36, 51, 116).

[98] A. Wood. „Software reliability growth models: assumptions vs. reality." In: *Software Reliability Engineering, 1997. Proceedings., The Eighth International Symposium on*. Nov. 1997, pp. 136–141 (cit. on p. 6).

The Karlsruhe Series on Software Design and Quality

Edited by Prof. Dr. Ralf Reussner // ISSN 1867-0067

Band 1 **Steffen Becker**
Coupled Model Transformations for QoS Enabled Component-Based Software Design.
ISBN 978-3-86644-271-9

Band 2 **Heiko Koziolek**
Parameter Dependencies for Reusable Performance Specifications of Software Components.
ISBN 978-3-86644-272-6

Band 3 **Jens Happe**
Predicting Software Performance in Symmetric Multi-core and Multiprocessor Environments.
ISBN 978-3-86644-381-5

Band 4 **Klaus Krogmann**
Reconstruction of Software Component Architectures and Behaviour Models using Static and Dynamic Analysis.
ISBN 978-3-86644-804-9

Band 5 **Michael Kuperberg**
Quantifying and Predicting the Influence of Execution Platform on Software Component Performance.
ISBN 978-3-86644-741-7

Band 6 **Thomas Goldschmidt**
View-Based Textual Modelling.
ISBN 978-3-86644-642-7

Band 7 **Anne Koziolek**
Automated Improvement of Software Architecture Models for Performance and Other Quality Attributes.
ISBN 978-3-86644-973-2

Die Bände sind unter www.ksp.kit.edu als PDF frei verfügbar oder als Druckausgabe bestellbar.

Band 8 **Lucia Happe**
Configurable Software Performance Completions through Higher-Order Model Transformations.
ISBN 978-3-86644-990-9

Band 9 **Franz Brosch**
Integrated Software Architecture-Based Reliability Prediction for IT Systems.
ISBN 978-3-86644-859-9

Band 10 **Christoph Rathfelder**
Modelling Event-Based Interactions in Component-Based Architectures for Quantitative System Evaluation.
ISBN 978-3-86644-969-5

Band 11 **Henning Groenda**
Certifying Software Component Performance Specifications.
ISBN 978-3-7315-0080-3

Band 12 **Dennis Westermann**
Deriving Goal-oriented Performance Models by Systematic Experimentation.
ISBN 978-3-7315-0165-7

Band 13 **Michael Hauck**
Automated Experiments for Deriving Performance-relevant Properties of Software Execution Environments.
ISBN 978-3-7315-0138-1

Band 14 **Zoya Durdik**
Architectural Design Decision Documentation through Reuse of Design Patterns.
ISBN 978-3-7315-0292-0

Band 15 **Erik Burger**
Flexible Views for View-based Model-driven Development.
ISBN 978-3-7315-0276-0

Band 16 **Benjamin Klatt**
Consolidation of Customized Product Copies into Software Product Lines.
ISBN 978-3-7315-0368-2

Band 17 **Andreas Rentschler**
Model Transformation Languages with Modular Information Hiding.
ISBN 978-3-7315-0346-0

Band 18 **Omar-Qais Noorshams**
Modeling and Prediction of I/O Performance in Virtualized Environments.
ISBN 978-3-7315-0359-0

Band 19 **Johannes Josef Stammel**
Architekturbasierte Bewertung und Planung von Änderungsanfragen.
ISBN 978-3-7315-0524-2

Band 20 **Alexander Wert**
Performance Problem Diagnostics by Systematic Experimentation.
ISBN 978-3-7315-0677-5

Band 21 **Christoph Heger**
An Approach for Guiding Developers to Performance and Scalability Solutions.
ISBN 978-3-7315-0698-0

Band 22 **Fouad ben Nasr Omri**
Weighted Statistical Testing based on Active Learning and Formal Verification Techniques for Software Reliability Assessment.
ISBN 978-3-7315-0472-6